Living in Provence
Vivre en Provence

Living in Provence
Vivre en Provence

Barbara & René Stoeltie

EDITED BY · HERAUSGEGEBEN VON · SOUS LA DIRECTION DE

Angelika Taschen

TASCHEN

KÖLN LONDON LOS ANGELES MADRID PARIS TOKYO

CONTENTS
INHALT
SOMMAIRE

JOHN BURNINGHAM & HELEN OXENBURY

Drôme provençale

It is impossible to cite the names John Burningham and Helen Oxenbury in anything other than one breath, for these two artists appear to be linked by an invisible umbilical cord. Over the years, Burningham and Oxenbury have established an international reputation as book illustrators. Few are those who, as children, did not pore over Helen's charming drawings in "We're Going on a Bear Hunt" or laughed themselves close to tears turning the pages of "John Burningham's France", John's mischievously funny portrait of the country both he and Helen adore. Not surprisingly, the couple's French home, which the Burningham-Oxenburys admit they spent a small fortune on restoring, echoes their personalities. John and Helen fell in love with the ruined country house nestling at the foot of Mont Ventoux, but it took great audacity and a vivid imagination to transform an old Provençal farm into a Tuscan villa. The couple boldly added a balcony, an 18th-century tower (bought from an antique dealer), new floors, a Hollywood-style pool and a loggia worthy of a Roman villa. Throughout the days and deliciously long evenings, Caruso's magical vocals issue from the papier-mâché funnel of a 1930s EMG gramophone, echoing through the surrounding vineyard. A perfect Provençal moment!

LEFT: *Next to the pool, Helen and John have built an 18th-century style pavilion.*

LINKS: *Neben dem Schwimmbecken ließen Helen und John ein Häuschen im Stil des 18. Jahrhunderts errichten.*

A GAUCHE: *Près de la piscine, Helen et John ont fait construire un pavillon 18e trompeusement authentique.*

Die Namen John Burningham und Helen Oxenbury getrennt zu nennen, erscheint geradezu unmöglich, so eng sind die beiden Künstler einander verbunden. Beide sind Buchillustratoren, und ihr überragendes Talent ist weltweit ein Begriff. Wer von uns hat nicht als Kind das von Helen illustrierte „Wir gehen auf Bärenjagd" gelesen oder Tränen über „John Burningham's France" gelacht, eine augenzwinkernde Hommage an das Land, das John und Helen so sehr lieben? Ihr Haus ist Spiegel ihrer Seele. Für die Restaurierung einer Ruine am Fuß des Mont Ventoux haben die beiden zugegebenermaßen ein Vermögen ausgegeben. Es gehört schon viel Mut und Ideenreichtum dazu, ein provençalisches Landhaus in eine toskanische Villa zu verwandeln, komplett mit neuem Balkon, einem Turm aus dem 18. Jahrhundert (den sie einem Fachmann für alte Baustoffe abkauften), neuen Dielenböden, einem Schwimmbecken und einer Loggia, die jedes römische Haus zieren würden. Die milden Tage und vor allem die langen Abende vergehen wie im Traum, während aus dem überdimensionalen Pappmaché-Trichter des EMG-Grammophons aus den 1930er Jahren Carusos unvergleichlicher Tenor über die nahen Weingärten weht.

The living-room, converted from a former barn, features an eye-catching staircase whose clear, vertical lines strikingly contrast with the rounded forms of this antique terracotta pot.

In der alten Scheune, dem heutigen Wohnraum, kontrastiert die geradlinige Treppe mit einer bauchigen alten Terrakottavase.

Dans l'ancienne grange transformée en séjour, l'escalier aux lignes épurées contraste avec les rondeurs d'un pot en terre cuite ancien.

Impossible de mentionner les noms de John Burningham et Helen Oxenbury séparément, tant il semble que ces artistes soient liés par un cordon ombilical invisible. Burningham et Oxenbury sont des illustrateurs de livres, et leur grand talent est reconnu dans le monde entier. Tout le monde ou presque a lu dans son enfance « La chasse à l'ours » – illustré par Helen – et ri aux larmes en parcourant les pages de la « France » de John Burningham, un portrait plein d'humour et de malice d'un pays que John et Helen adorent. Et la maison qu'ils y possèdent fait écho à leur personnalité. Les Burningham-Oxenbury avouent qu'ils ont dépensé une somme ridicule pour restaurer une maison de campagne en ruine au pied du Mont Ventoux. Il faut de l'audace et de l'inventivité pour transformer une grande ferme provençale en villa toscane en y ajoutant un balcon, une tour 18e (achetée chez un marchand de matériaux anciens) des planchers neufs, une piscine hollywoodienne et une loggia digne d'une villa romaine. Mais les jours et les – longues – soirées y sont douces, le gramophone EMG des années 1930 fait sortir la belle voix de Caruso de son cornet en papier mâché démesuré et les vignes environnantes forment un décor de rêve.

Oriental embroidery wall-hangings and a flowerpot holder in Moustiers faience add a touch of colour to the vast space and austere décor of the living-room.

Exotische Wandteppiche und ein Fayence-Blumentopf aus Moustiers beleben das strenge Dekor der Wohnhalle.

Des broderies orientales et un cache-pot en faïence de Moustiers égayent le décor austère du vaste séjour.

PREVIOUS PAGES:
Behind the house, the vineyard stretches away to the horizon bathed in a soft, Provençal glow reminiscent of Tuscany.
RIGHT: *The masters of the house indulge their eclectic taste for décor, juxtaposing a magnificent refectory table with a pot from Les Anduzes and a Victorian armchair. In winter, a cosy logfire roars in the vast stone hearth.*

VORHERGEHENDE
DOPPELSEITE: *Hinter dem Haus erstrecken sich endlose Weingärten. Die Provence erscheint hier in den Farben der Toskana.*
RECHTS: *Ein massiver Refektoriumstisch, ein Anduze-Topf und ein viktorianischer Sessel belegen den eklektischen Geschmack der Hausbesitzer. Im Winter sorgt der riesige offene Kamin für behagliche Wärme.*

DOUBLE PAGE PRE-
CEDENTE: *Des vignes s'étendent à perte de vue derrière la maison. Ici la Provence emprunte les couleurs de la Toscane.*
A DROITE: *Une magnifique table de réfectoire, un pot des Anduzes et un fauteuil victorien révèlent le goût éclectique des maîtres de maison. En hiver, la grande cheminée répand une chaleur réconfortante.*

LEFT: *Tucked away in a corner of the living room, next to the main window, Helen and John like to unwind listening to original recordings by Gigli, Caruso and Chaliapine. The delicate old-rose hue of the gramophone horn is echoed in the colours of the neighbouring armchair and lampshade.*
FACING PAGE: *An embroidered Art Deco cushion draws the eye to an elegant three-seater sofa upholstered in damask. The mirror gives the room an added sense of depth.*

LINKS: *In einer Ecke des Wohnraums, nahe dem Fenster, entspannen sich Helen und John zu Originalaufnahmen von Gigli, Caruso und Schaljapin. Sessel und Lampenschirm greifen das Altrosa des Grammophontrichters auf.*
RECHTE SEITE: *Ein Stickkissen im Art-Déco-Stil lenkt den Blick auf die mit feinem Damast bezogene große Couch. Der Spiegel täuscht Raumtiefe vor.*

A GAUCHE: *C'est dans un coin de séjour près de la grande fenêtre que Helen et John écoutent la musique et les enregistrements originaux de Gigli, Caruso ou de Chaliapine. La corne du gramophone prête sa couleur vieux rose au fauteuil et à l'abat-jour.*
PAGE DE DROITE: *Un coussin brodé typiquement Art Déco se love dans le vaste canapé houssé d'un tissu damassé. Le grand miroir donne une illusion de profondeur.*

CHATEAU DE MASSILLAN

Peter Wylly & Birgit Israël

Uchaux

The Château de Massillan stands in a picturesque Côtes du Rhône vineyard, a short distance from the ancient Roman town of Orange, its crenellated towers dramatically silhouetted against the horizon. In 1550 Massillan belonged to Diane de Poitiers, the beautiful huntress who was the mistress of King Henri II, but three years ago the castle and surrounding grounds were bought by a trio of modern entrepreneurs. Peter Wylly and Birgit Israël, a couple of designers who sell their creations through their London-based company Babylon Design Ltd. teamed up with renowned German chef Marc Koenemund to create a "high-class" hotel-restaurant. The trio have favoured understated luxury in their stylish décor, avoiding design stereotypes, although this does not mean Peter and Birgit are averse to the idea of period furniture and fittings, or have banned crystal chandeliers (a feature inevitably associated with luxury hotels). These classic touches are complemented by minimalist forms, pastel tones and a sober style of modern chic which, together with Marc Koenemund's sophisticated cuisine, make the Château de Massillan a truly exclusive address.

LEFT: *A crystal chandelier is set off against the dark backdrop of a curtain. The décor at the Château de Massillan is a perfect mix of chic and sobriety.*

LINKS: *Ein Kristallüster glitzert vor dem dunklen Vorhang. Das Château de Massillan paart Perfektion mit nüchterner Eleganz.*

A GAUCHE: *Un chandelier en cristal se détache sur le rideau sombre. Le Château de Massillan marie à la perfection chic et sobriété.*

Im Herzen des Weinanbaugebiets Côtes du Rhône, nicht weit von Orange und seinen antiken Kunstschätzen entfernt, taucht unvermittelt die imposante Silhouette des Château de Massillan mit seinen dicken, zinnenbewehrten Türmen auf. 1550 gehörte es der schönen Jägerin Diane de Poitiers, die König Heinrich II. in ihren Bann zu ziehen verstand. Vor drei Jahren übernahm ein geschäftstüchtiges Trio den gesamten Besitz: Gemeinsam mit dem renommierten deutschen Küchenchef Marc Koenemund machten Peter Wylly und Birgit Israël – zwei Designer, die ihre Kreationen über ihre Firma Babylon Design Ltd. in London vertreiben – aus dem Anwesen ein Luxushotel mit Gourmetrestaurant. Doch der Luxus hier ist von erlesener Zurückhaltung, denn stereotype Lösungen liegen den dreien ganz und gar nicht. Das heißt keineswegs, dass Peter und Birgit etwas gegen Stilmöbel, klassische Wandleuchten oder glitzernde Kronleuchter hätten, denn solche Accessoires gehören nun einmal in jedes Schloss. Doch sie verliehen dem Château de Massillan darüber hinaus mit klaren, prägnanten Formen und Pastelltönen eine exquisite Schlichtheit, mit der Koenemunds raffiniertes Küchenangebot ausgezeichnet harmoniert.

In the stairwell, the wrought-iron wall sconces echo the design of the banister whose elegant filigree work curves gracefully up-stairs.

Die schmiedeeiserne Wandleuchte im Treppenhaus harmoniert mit dem filigranen Geländer an der Treppe zum ersten Stock.

Dans la cage d'escalier, l'applique en fer forgé fait écho à la superbe rampe qui orne l'escalier en pierre menant à l'étage.

Situé au cœur du vignoble des Côtes du Rhône et à une distance agréable de l'antique cité d'Orange, la silhouette imposante du Château de Massillan, avec ses robustes tours à créneaux, surgit devant l'œil surpris du visiteur. Ayant appartenu en 1550 à Diane de Poitiers, la belle chasseresse qui sut s'assurer la passion du roi Henri II, le château et son domaine furent achetés il y a trois ans par un trio entreprenant : Peter Wylly et Birgit Israël, un couple de designers qui éditent leurs créations par l'intermédiaire de leur firme Babylon Design Ltd., implantée à Londres et Marc Koenemund, un chef allemand réputé, avaient envie de créer un hôtel-restaurant « grand luxe ». Toutefois Wylly, Israël et Könemund prônent un luxe qui ne se fait pas remarquer. Les solutions stéréotypes ne les intéressaient pas. Ce qui ne veut pas dire que Peter et Birgit soient allergiques aux meubles de style, aux appliques classiques et aux lustres en cristal qui seront pour toujours associés à l'idée que l'on se fait des palaces. Mais en imposant au Château de Massillan des formes épurées, des tons pastel, une sobriêté de décoration exclusive et la cuisine raffinée de Koenemund, ils on gagné leur pari.

This imposing castle, guarded by fortress-style walls and resonant with the spirit of Diane de Poitiers, will appeal to those of a romantic bent.

Schloss oder Festung? Der einstige Wohnsitz von Diane de Poitiers ist ein Traum für die Romantiker unter uns.

Ce château aux allures de forteresse, qui abrite le souvenir de Diane de Poitiers ne peut que plaire aux esprits romantiques.

Off-white walls and pale stone set off period furniture and modern sofas upholstered in simple shades. Peter Wylly and Birgit Israël have adopted an elegantly restrained colour scheme.

Gebrochen weiße Wände, hellgelber Stein und gedämpfte Dekostoffe als Bezüge von Stilmöbeln und modernen Sofas: Die von Peter Wylly und Birgit Israël gewählte Farbpalette ist von einzigartiger Schlichtheit.

Murs blanc cassé, pierres blondes et nuances discrètes des tissus qui recouvrent le mobilier de style et les canapés contemporains. La palette choisie par Peter Wylly et Birgit Israël est d'une sobriété exemplaire.

FACING PAGE: *Interior accessories have been chosen with the same attention to minimalist line and form. Positioned in the corner of one of the bedrooms, this standard lamp is a striking example of the house style.*
RIGHT: *This spacious gallery, leading off the courtyard, is filled with rattan armchairs and miniature lemon trees, tastefully juxtaposed with a more classic style of antique furniture.*

LINKE SEITE: *Jedes Detail zeigt die gleiche Liebe zu schnörkellosen Formen und Linien. Diese Stehlampe aus einem der Hotelzimmer ist ein eindrucksvolles Beispiel dafür.*
RECHTS: *Auf der großen Veranda am Ende des Hofs wechseln sich Rattansessel und Zitronenbäumchen mit klassisch geschwungenen Sitzgruppen ab.*

PAGE DE GAUCHE: *Les accessoires témoignent de la même affinité pour les formes et les lignes épurées. Dans une des chambres, un pied de lampe et son abat-jour en sont un exemple frappant.*
A DROITE: *Dans la grande galerie située au fond de la cour, des fauteuils en rotin et des citronniers en pot alternent avec des fauteuils et des canapés aux formes classiques.*

The bedrooms, fur-
nished with impeccable
taste, exude the same
understated luxury as
'hôtels particuliers' of
the 1930s and 40s. But
every effort has been
made to assure 21st-
century comfort.

Die liebevoll möblier-
ten Zimmer verströmen
eine Aura von Luxus
und Diskretion, wie sie
die großen privaten
Palais der 1930er und
40er Jahre besaßen.
Dabei wird natürlich
jeglichem modernen
Komfort Rechnung ge-
tragen.

Les chambres meublées
avec le plus grand soin
possèdent l'ambiance
luxueuse et discrète
des grands hôtels parti-
culiers des années 1930
et 40. Et le confort si
cher aux hommes du
21e siècle.

LEFT: *Sober black-and-white décor dominates in the dining room. Peter Wylly and Birgit Israël were determined guests' attention should not be distracted from the 'haute cuisine.'*

FACING PAGE: *Bathed in natural light from the dining-room window, the dark curtains frame an elegant still life of earthenware soup tureens posed on a white linen tablecloth.*

LINKS: *Das Restaurant hielten Peter Wylly und Birgit Israël in strengem Schwarz-Weiß, damit sich die Gäste ganz auf die raffinierten Speisen konzentrieren können.*

RECHTE SEITE: *Am Fenster des Speisesaals umrahmen dunkle Vorhänge ein Stillleben aus Fayence-Suppenterrinen auf schneeweißem Leinentischtuch.*

A GAUCHE: *ambiance noir et blanc stricte pour la salle à manger. Peter Wylly et Birgit Israël n'ont pas voulu distraire l'attention de leurs hôtes de la cuisine raffinée.*

PAGE DE DROITE: *Près de la fenêtre de la salle à manger, les rideaux sombres se lèvent sur une nature morte composée d'une table drapée de lin blanc et de quelques soupières en faïence.*

The simple, sober style of the furniture accentuates the architectural austerity and minimalist inspiration that is also in evidence in the bathrooms. Here, the ochre charms of Provence are kept to the exterior.

Die Schlichtheit des Mobiliars unterstreicht die nüchterne Bauweise. Der gleiche minimalistische Geschmack findet sich in den Bädern. Hier wartet der ockergelbe Charme der Provence draußen vor der Tür.

Le dépouillement du mobilier accentue l'austérité de l'architecture. On retrouve la même inspiration minimaliste dans les salles de bains. Ici la Provence ocrée ne « chante » qu'au-delà de la fenêtre.

$\mathcal{L}$A MIRANDE

La famille Stein

Avignon

A decade ago La Mirande, the stylish 'hôtel particulier' which stands in a tranquil cobbled square at the foot of the Palais des Papes in Avignon, opened its imposing doors embellished with grotesque masks. Since then, guests from all over the world have stayed in this magnificent residence, tastefully restored and decorated by the Stein family. Expressing their passion for the decorative arts and architecture of the 18th century, Achim and Hannelore Stein and their son, Martin, worked in close collaboration with the interior decorator François Joseph Graff. The Steins sought to make their restoration of the former Hôtel Pamard as authentic as possible and, at the same time, create a warm and welcoming atmosphere. The family wanted guests to feel as if they were staying in the home of an old family from the Provençal aristocracy. The luxuriously comfortable interiors feature period furniture, wood panelling, floral wallpaper, beautiful engravings and rustic pieces of earthenware. Needless to say, La Mirande has established a reputation as one of the most upmarket destinations in Avignon. And, while the Steins may be too modest to boast about their unique creation, under the impeccable management of their son, Martin, La Mirande looks set to become a great classic.

LEFT: *The gardener tends his charges with loving care, pruning the sumptuous white roses that bloom in the walled garden at La Mirande.*

LINKS: *Ein geschickter Gärtner weiß, was Pflanzen gut tut: Liebevoll werden hier die weißen Rosen im Hotelgarten umsorgt.*

A GAUCHE: *Attentif aux besoins des plantes, le jardinier s'occupe avec amour des roses blanches du jardin muré de la Mirande.*

Zehn Jahre ist es schon her, seit La Mirande seine mit skurrilen Masken verzierten Pforten öffnete. Seither haben Gäste aus aller Welt das Hotel zu Füßen des Papstpalastes in Avignon besucht, das mit so viel Liebe zum Detail und Begeisterung für die Architektur und das Kunsthandwerk des 18. Jahrhunderts neu gestaltet wurde. Um den Stil möglichst authentisch nachzubilden, ließen sich Achim, Hannelore und Martin Stein bei der Restaurierung des ehemaligen Hôtel Pamard von dem Innenarchitekten François Joseph Graff beraten. Am Herzen lag ihnen vor allem, dem vornehmen Stadthaus eine warme, einladende Atmosphäre zu verleihen. Da die Steins selbst für die Provence schwärmen, wollten sie auch ihren Gästen das Gefühl vermitteln, bei einer alten provençalischen Adelsfamilie zu Gast zu sein: Die komfortablen Zimmer sind mit Stilmöbeln, Holzvertäfelungen und romantischen Tapeten ausgestattet, ergänzt durch gemusterte Indienne-Stoffe, Stiche und rustikale Fayencen. La Mirande gehört zu Recht zu den ersten Häusern Avignons, wenn nicht sogar der Welt. Ihr Hotel unter der geschickten Regie von Sohn Martin hat gute Chancen, ein echter Klassiker zu werden.

This narrow corridor, leading to one of the bathrooms, is decorated with a rustic chair and an 18th-century engraving set off against the floral wallpaper.

Ein rustikaler Stuhl und ein Stich aus dem 18. Jahrhundert auf farbenfroher Tapete leiten im Korridor zu einem der Bäder.

Dans un passage étroit qui mène vers une salle de bains, une chaise rustique et une gravure 18e sur fond de papier peint.

Dix ans déjà que La Mirande a ouvert ses portes imposantes ornées de mascarons au pied du Palais des Papes à Avignon. Depuis, des hôtes du monde entier ont séjourné dans ce bel hôtel particulier restauré et décoré par la famille Stein avec un goût et un souci du détail qui révèlent leur passion pour l'architecture et les arts décoratifs du 18e siècle. Guidés dans leur recherche de l'authenticité par le décorateur François Joseph Graff, Achim et Hannelore Stein et leur fils Martin ont restauré l'ancien Hôtel Pamard avec l'intention d'y créer une ambiance chaleureuse et accueillante. Amoureux de la Provence, ils désiraient que leurs hôtes aient l'impression de séjourner chez une de ces vieilles familles de l'aristocratie provençale, dans un intérieur confortable, entourés de meubles d'époque, de lambris et de papiers peints fleuris, le tout enjolivé par la présence d'indiennes, de gravures et de belles faïences rustiques. La Mirande, faut-il s'en étonner, est devenue un haut lieu d'Avignon et une révélation dans le monde hôtelier. Les Stein sont trop modestes pour s'en féliciter, mais sous la baguette magique de leur fils Martin leur création unique a toutes les chances de devenir un grand classique.

Tucked away in a tiny sitting-room on the ground floor, this period armchair makes a perfect refuge in which to languish and daydream.

Im kleinen Salon des Erdgeschosses lädt ein geschmackvoller Sessel zum Ausruhen und Träumen ein.

Dans le petit salon du rez-de-chaussée, un siège de style invite à la détente et aux rêveries.

PAGES 28–31: *La Mirande impresses with the sheer quality of its restoration and the unique charm of its interior, where a multitude of period details have been painstakingly preserved.*

FACING PAGE: *In the cosy living room, set aside for intimate dinners, a huge glass-fronted cupboard displays a stunning collection of 18th-century crockery.*

SEITE 28–31: *La Mirande bezaubert durch die Qualität der Küche, den einzigartigen Charme der Einrichtung und die vielen sorgsam gehüteten Kleinigkeiten von anno dazumal.*

RECHTE SEITE: *In dem für kleine Tischgesellschaften reservierten Salon steht ein wunderschönes Service aus dem 18. Jahrhundert in einer Vitrine.*

PAGES 28–31: *La Mirande enchante par la qualité de la restauration, le charme unique de son intérieur et par une multitude de détails d'époque jalousement préservés.*

A DROITE: *Dans le salon destiné aux dîners intimes, une armoire vitrée de dimensions généreuses abrite une splendide vaisselle 18ᵉ.*

LEFT: *Every Friday, Martin Stein hosts a dinner which pays rich homage to the local cuisine. Here, the renowned chef prepares a delicious Provençal dish.*

FACING PAGE: *La Mirande features the most sumptuous design details. The restaurant is hung with a 17th-century Flemish tapestry.*

LINKS: *Freitags lädt Martin Stein zu einem Gastessen, das eine echte Liebeserklärung an die provençalische Küche ist. Das Gericht, das der renommierte Küchenchef hier zubereitet, verströmt die delikaten Aromen dieser einmaligen Landschaft.*

RECHTE SEITE: *La Mirande steht auch für prächtiges Dekor. So hängt im Restaurant ein flämischer Wandteppich aus dem 17. Jahrhundert.*

A GAUCHE: *Tous les vendredis, Martin Stein préside une table d'hôte qui est un véritable hommage à la cuisine provençale. Ici, le chef renommé prépare un plat délicieux aux arômes de Provence.*

PAGE DE DROITE: *La Mirande abonde aussi de détails somptueux : dans la salle de restaurant une tapisserie flamande 17ᵉ.*

PREVIOUS PAGES:
In the rustic kitchen in the basement, this massive beechwood table is set for a Provençal feast.
LEFT: *This Empire-style panel in one of the bedrooms was inspired by the treasures of Roman antiquity and excavations at Pompeii.*
FACING PAGE: *The same attention to period detail is evident in the reception room. This terracotta statuette of a shepherdess from 1900 is set off against wood panelling in Louis XVI-style.*

VORHERGEHENDE DOPPELSEITE: *In der Küche im Souterrain genießen die Gäste an einem langen Buchentisch provençalische Köstlichkeiten.*
LINKS: *Die klassizistischen Bildtapeten in einem der Zimmer haben altrömische Motive und Wandmalereien aus Pompeji zum Vorbild.*
RECHTE SEITE: *Auch der Empfangssalon ist mit viel Liebe zum zeitgenössischen Detail gestaltet. Das bukolische Tonfigürchen aus der Zeit um 1900 harmoniert perfekt mit der Vertäfelung im Louis-XVI-Stil.*

DOUBLE PAGE PRE-CEDENTE: *Dans la cuisine du sous-sol, la grande table en hêtre attend ceux qui se laisseront séduire par la cuisine provençale.*
A GAUCHE: *Une des chambres a été tendue de panneaux de style Empire inspirés par les fouilles de Pompéi et par l'antiquité romaine.*
PAGE DE DROITE: *Le même soin du détail d'époque se reflète dans le salon. Une statuette de bergère d'époque 1900 en terre cuite se marie avec des boiseries dans le style Louis XVI.*

GERALD BEAUME

Avignon

Being an antique dealer in the 21st century requires not only a practised and experienced eye, but a fair amount of audacity, too. It's not just a question of plunging your hands into the cornucopia of last century's design in the hope of pulling up a precious lamp, rare carpet or piece of furniture possessed of timeless value. Gérald Beaume appears to have an innate knack for spotting the perfect piece with the greatest of ease, plumping straight for a stylish sofa by Danish designer Finn Juhl or a chair by Hans J. Wegner. Beaume's modest-sized Avignon boutique is filled with upmarket products of French 1950s design and intriguing Danish models from the 60s with a Japanese influence. But it is in his apartment, situated in a narrow street a stone's throw from Les Halles, that he has created the perfect Zen ambience to show off the pieces he cannot bear to part with. Set against a floor of varnished red hexagonal tiles and a backdrop of pure white walls (reminiscent of the gloss paint so dear to Le Corbusier), Beaume has assembled an eclectic collection which includes a Pierre Paulin desk, an array of 60s carpets and a plane propeller. No doubt, these avant-garde designs of the past are set to become tomorrow's classics.

LEFT: *The discreetly positioned bell signals that visitors are about to enter a "temple" dedicated to art.*
PAGES 42–43: *In the living room, Isamu Noguchi's famous coffee table makes a design statement alongside Richard Sapper's "Tizio" lamp and a typical 1960s 'chaise longue' by Olivier Mourgue.*

LINKS: *Schon die Klingel neben der Eingangstür signalisiert, dass sich im Inneren alles um Kunst dreht.*
SEITE 42–43: *Im Wohnzimmer steht Isamu Noguchis berühmter Couchtisch neben Richard Sappers Lampe „Tizio" und einer für die 1960er Jahre typischen Liege von Olivier Mourgue.*

A GAUCHE: *A côté de la porte d'entrée, la sonnette avertit que l'intérieur sera voué à l'art.*
PAGES 42–43: *Dans le séjour, la célèbre table basse d'Isamu Noguchi côtoie la lampe « Tizio » signée Richard Sapper et une chaise longue typiquement « sixties » créée par Olivier Mourgue.*

Um als Antiquitätenhändler im 21. Jahrhundert erfolgreich zu sein, braucht man nicht nur Erfahrung und einen Kennerblick, sondern auch eine gehörige Portion Mut. Nur dann fördert der beherzte Griff ins Füllhorn des letzten Jahrhunderts hochwertige Möbelstücke, Lampen oder Teppiche zutage, nur dann entdeckt man Kostbarkeiten, die sich im Nachhinein als zeitlos erweisen. Gérald Beaume gehört zu jenen, die ohne zu zögern ein Kanapee des Dänen Finn Juhl oder einen Hans-J.-Wegner-Stuhl auswählen. Seine eher kleinen Geschäftsräume in Avignon bieten unter anderem hochwertige französische Objekte aus den 1950er Jahren und dänische Stücke im Japan-Look aus den 60ern. In seiner eigenen Wohnung in einer schmalen Seitenstraße unweit der Markthallen kann sich das Auge erholen. In diesem vom Zen-Geist geprägten Ambiente inszeniert er seine liebsten Stücke. Vor den weißen Wänden (die an die von Le Corbusier so geschätzte Lackfarbe erinnern) harmonieren ein Pierre-Paulin-Schreibtisch, Teppiche aus den 60er Jahren und ein Flugzeugpropeller mühelos mit den glasierten Terrakotta-Bodenfliesen. Hier wird deutlich: Was gestern noch Avantgarde-Design war, kann morgen schon zu den Klassikern zählen.

Gérald Beaume is not one to be overawed by the "big names" of the design world. The ceramics displayed here were chosen for their aesthetic qualities alone.

Für Gérald Beaume zählen nicht nur die „prominenten Namen" des Designs. Diese Keramiken wählte er allein auf Grund ihres ästhetischen Wertes.

Gérald Beaume n'est guère impressionné par les « grandes signatures » du design. Ici les céramiques n'ont été choisies que pour leur esthétique.

Etre antiquaire au 21e siècle, voilà qui demande un regard perçant et exercé ainsi qu'une bonne dose de courage. Il ne suffit pas en effet de plonger la main dans la corne d'abondance du design du siècle dernier pour en sortir le meuble, la lampe ou le tapis de qualité et de dénicher des trouvailles qui se distingueront ensuite par leur valeur intemporelle. Gérald Beaume, lui, ne connaît nulle hésitation et choisit un canapé du Danois Finn Juhl ou une chaise de Hans J. Wegner. Sa boutique avignonnaise – de dimensions modestes – est remplie, entre autres de réalisations « fifties » haut de gamme françaises et de « sixties » danoises au profil japonisant. Mais c'est dans son appartement, situé dans une rue étroite à deux pas des Halles, qu'il retrouve la paix visuelle et l'ambiance « zen » qui lui permettent de mettre en scène des pièces dont il hésite à se séparer. Sur fond de murs blancs (souvenons-nous du Ripolin cher à Le Corbusier !), un bureau de Pierre Paulin, des tapis des années 1960 et une hélice d'avion font bon ménage avec un sol en tomettes rouges vernies. Ici, on peut s'imaginer sans peine qu'un jour le design d'avant-garde d'hier, deviendra le grand classique de demain.

The bedroom is dominated by a 70s rug and a mattress covered with a bedspread inspired by the distinctive art of Joseph Beuys.

Dieses Zimmer bietet nur Platz für einen Bettvorleger aus den 70ern und die Matratze unter einem von Joseph Beuys inspirierten Bettüberwurf.

Dans cette chambre à coucher, il n'y a de la place que pour une carpette «seventies» et un matelas qui disparaît sous un couvre-lit inspiré par l'art unique de Joseph Beuys.

MICHELLE &
YVES HALARD

Le Thor

"I loathe decoration!" Michelle Halard declares. Throughout her long and successful career as an interior decorator and designer of textiles, household linens, lamps and tableware, this remarkable woman has defended the anti-décor movement to the hilt, promoting a return to the simple values of the family home. "I'm totally disorganised," Michelle insists, although her designs utterly refute her claims, and the interiors she has created with her husband, Yves, exude a calm sense of spontaneity and well-being. The Halards claim to have lived in Paris "for ever," but they had never given up on the idea of finding a second home in Provence. Leaving their magnificent 'château' in the Berry region, the couple set off on a quest of the South. And a long and eventful quest it turned out to be, as they trawled through "all those 'renovated' houses and 'modern' bathrooms tiled with daisy motifs that didn't appeal to us at all." One day, the Halards came across a dilapidated 18th-century farmhouse which let them exercise their talent for transforming a rustic ruin into a charming home, filled with a delightful assortment of furniture, treasured objects and family souvenirs arranged with the couple's orderly nonchalance.

LEFT: *The house has retained its period wrought ironwork and the Halards have kept to a subdued 18th-century colour scheme, keeping the house as close as possible to its original hues.*

LINKS: *Das Haus besitzt noch die alten Fenstergitter. Bei der Farbwahl entschieden sich die Halards für zarte Töne, die den ursprünglichen Nuancen nachempfunden sind.*

A GAUCHE: *La maison a gardé ses ferronneries d'époque. Et côté couleur, les Halard ont choisi une délicate palette 18ᵉ qui se rapproche des teintes originales.*

„Ich hasse Dekorationen!", verkündet Michelle Halard, und es stimmt: Während ihrer Laufbahn als Innenarchitektin und Designerin von Stoffen und Lampen über Bett- und Tischwäsche bis hin zu Tafelgeschirr hat sie stets vehement die Vorzüge der „Anti-Dekoration" verteidigt. Ihr Ideal ist das gemütliche Zuhause. „Ich bin sehr unordentlich", behauptet diese bemerkenswerte Frau, doch ihre Kreationen beweisen das Gegenteil. Die gemeinsam mit Ehemann Yves gestalteten Interieurs zeichnen sich durch Spontaneität und Behaglichkeit aus. Beide wohnen zwar „immer schon" in Paris, träumen jedoch ebenso lange von einem zweiten Wohnsitz in der Provence. Von ihrem Schloss im Berry aus eroberten sie Südfrankreich. Die rastlose Suche war zunächst eher enttäuschend: „All die ‚renovierten' Häuser und ‚modernen' Bäder mit ihren Blümchenfliesen überzeugten uns nicht im Geringsten." Das tat erst ein großes, halb zerfallenes Bauernhaus aus dem 18. Jahrhundert; es bot den Halards Gelegenheit, erneut ihr einzigartiges Talent zu beweisen: Aus einer Ruine machten sie ein Haus voller bunt zusammengewürfelter Möbel, charmanter Accessoires und Andenken, das die für sie typische Atmosphäre wohl geordneter Lässigkeit verströmt.

Michelle has arranged a set of classic garden furniture in front of the house. The tablecloth is an ingenious reinvention of an old linen bedsheet dyed eye-catching pink.

Vor dem Haus stellte Michelle klassische Gartenmöbel auf. Als Tischdecke dient ein schönes altes Betttuch in leuchtendem Rosa.

Michelle a installé devant sa maison des meubles de jardin classiques. La nappe n'est autre qu'un drap de lit ancien teint en rose vif.

« Je déteste la décoration ! » s'exclame Michelle Halard. De fait, tout au long de sa carrière de décoratrice et de créatrice de tissus, de lampes, de linge de maison et de services de table, personne n'a mieux défendu les bienfaits de l'anti-décoration et de la maison de famille, chaleureuse et accueillante. « Je suis désordonnée » ajoute cette femme remarquable dont les réalisations démentent ces propos et qui a signé avec son mari Yves des intérieurs marqués par la spontanéité et le sens du bien-être. Installés à Paris « depuis toujours », les Halard n'avaient jamais abandonné l'idée d'une seconde résidence en Provence. Ils ont quitté leur magnifique château du Berry pour partir à la conquête du Midi. Conquête mouvementée et déprimante car « toutes les maisons 'rénovées' et toutes ces salles de bains 'modernes' décorées avec des carrelages aux motif de pâquerettes n'avaient rien pour nous plaire ». En revanche une grande maison de cultivateurs 18e, en très mauvais état, leur a permis de prouver à nouveau leur don unique de transformer une ruine en une maison remplie de meubles hétéroclites, d'objets charmants et de souvenirs de famille et où règne une nonchalance ordonnée caractéristique.

An 18th-century staircase and tiled floor. The Halards have not altered the house's original architecture or period features.

Bodenfliesen und Treppe aus dem 18. Jahrhundert wurden wie auch die Architektur und zeitgenössische Details von den Halards nicht angetastet.

Sol à dallages et cage d'escalier 18e: Les Halard n'ont pas touché à l'architecture et aux détails d'époque.

PREVIOUS PAGE: *Michelle Halard knows how to preserve her houses intact. It is imposing but full of rustic charm. Despite new colourwash on the walls and a fresh coat of paint on the shutters, the house retains its original soul.*
RIGHT: *The sunflower-yellow living room is furnished with sumptuous Napoleon III armchairs, antique chairs, designer stools and quirky garden gnomes designed by Philippe Starck. The look is totally "Halard," yet totally Provence.*

VORHERGEHENDE DOPPELSEITE: *Bei allem Glanz ist das Haus durchaus rustikal, denn Michelle Halard belässt alte Häuser intakt. Auch ein frischer Anstrich und neu lackierte Fensterläden nehmen ihrem Heim nichts vom Charme vergangener Tage.*
RECHTS: *Im sonnengelben Wohnraum stehen Polstersessel im Stil Napoleons III. und schöne alte Stühle neben Designerhockern und den kecken Gartenzwergen von Philippe Starck. Der Effekt ist „typisch Halard" und doch provençalisch.*

DOUBLE PAGE PRECEDENTE: *La maison est à la fois grandiose et rustique. Et Michelle Halard sait laisser ses maisons intactes. En dépit d'un nouveau badigeon et des volets repeints, la demeure a gardé son charme d'antan.*
A DROITE: *Le séjour jaune tournesol abrite des fauteuils capitonnés Napoléon III, des chaises de style, des tabourets design et de charmants gnomes signés Philippe Starck. Le résultat est indéniablement « Halard » et indiscutablement provençal.*

JEAN & DOROTHEE D'ORGEVAL

Roussillon

Jean and Dorothée d'Orgevals' home began life as a simple farmhouse and pigsty. Coming across this rustic abode, hidden away in a shady alleyway in the heart of Roussillon, the couple of antique dealers instantly recognised its potential and set about transforming it into a sophisticated and elegant holiday home. One of the house's most striking features is the warm ochre tones of the walls. Roussillon is internationally famous for its rich red earth, and the d'Orgevals took advantage of the local colour, mixing the pigment with their whitewash. Arriving in the garden, visitors will discover that the house, perched high on a hill, is surrounded by rocks whose rugged red hues echo the rich palette in the house's interior. The d'Orgevals' décor provides a perfect backdrop to the sturdy Provençal furniture, as well as to a magnificent Louis XIII couch and a sumptuous bed from the same period hung with a Hungarian-point tapestry are complimented by an impressive collection of faïences from Apt. The mistress of the house was responsible for the stunning 'trompe-l'œil' frescos in the bathroom and is equally famous for the succulent feasts she cooks up on the grill. Living in Provence with the d'Orgevals is not just a lifestyle; it's a veritable art!

LEFT: *A traditional logfire blazes in the massive stone hearth. Spring evenings in Provence can often be chilly.*

LINKS: *Im offenen Kamin knistert und knackt ein behagliches Feuer, denn die Frühlingsabende in der Provence sind oft frisch.*

A GAUCHE: *Un grand feu de bois crépite dans l'âtre de la vaste cheminée. En Provence, les soirées de printemps sont souvent fraîches.*

Gut versteckt im Schatten einer Gasse mitten in Roussillon stand einst ein großer Bauernhof mit Schweinestall. Jean und Dorothée d'Orgeval, ihres Zeichens Antiquitätenhändler, fanden ihn so imponierend, dass sie das rustikale Anwesen in ein Wohnhaus von raffinierter Eleganz verwandelten. Wer die Schwelle zu ihrem Ferienhaus heute überschreitet, ist angenehm überrascht vom warmen Ockerton der Wände. Das Pigment für die Kalkfarbe fanden Jean und Dorothée in der rötlich gelben Erde, für die Roussillon weltweit berühmt ist. Ihr Haus steht auf einer Hügelkuppe, und vom Garten aus blickt man ringsum auf Felsen, deren Töne der schillernden Farbpalette der Hausbesitzer in nichts nachstehen. Wände und Böden bilden einen geglückten Rahmen für das prächtige Louis-XIII-Kanapee, in der Ecke des Salons das Prunkbett aus derselben Epoche mit Tapisserien aus ungarischer Stickerei, extravagante Federbüsche und die beachtliche Sammlung von Fayencen aus Apt. Die Trompe-l'œil-Fresken im Bad stammen von der Hausherrin selbst – ebenso wie die Köstlichkeiten vom Grill, die für das leibliche Wohl der Gäste sorgen. Provençalisches Lebensgefühl ist im Haus d'Orgeval viel mehr als nur ein Stil: Es ist eine Kunst.

A bouquet of dried branches artfully arranged in an antique vase make a striking cornerpiece.

Ein paar Zweige genügen, um aus einer schönen, klassisch geformten Vase ein Stillleben zu gestalten.

Quelques branches esquissent une nature morte dans un joli vase aux formes classiques.

At the bottom of the garden, a flagstone path winds down to the old stone wall. From this archway, the d'Orgevals have a magnificent vista across the extraordinary panorama.

Hinten im Garten führt eine Allee zu einer uralten Mauer. Vom Fenster aus genießen die d'Orgeval einen zauberhaften Blick.

Au bout du jardin une allée mène vers un vieux mur. De la fenêtre, les d'Orgeval ont une vue époustouflante.

A l'origine, c'était une grande ferme avec porcherie cachée à l'ombre d'une ruelle au cœur de Roussillon. Les antiquaires Jean et Dorothée d'Orgeval lui ont trouvé si fière allure qu'ils n'ont pas hésité à transformer cette demeure rustique en une maison élégante et raffinée. Poussant la porte de leur maison de vacances, le visiteur est agréablement surpris par le ton ocre des murs. Roussillon, mondialement célèbre pour sa terre rousse, a fourni à Jean et Dorothée le pigment qu'ils ont mélangé à la chaux. En se dirigeant vers le jardin, on découvre que la maison, située au sommet d'une colline, est entourée de rochers qui font écho à la palette chatoyante des maîtres de maison. Le décor se marie à merveille avec le mobilier robuste, typiquement provençal et avec un magnifique canapé Louis XIII, un lit d'apparat de la même époque habillé d'une tapisserie au point de Hongrie, qui occupe un coin du séjour, de frivoles panaches et une collection impressionnante de faïences d'Apt. C'est à la maîtresse de maison qu'on doit les fresques en trompe-l'œil dans la salle de bains ainsi que les repas succulents préparés sur le gril. Vivre en Provence, chez les d'Orgeval est beaucoup plus qu'une expression. C'est un art.

PREVIOUS PAGES: *The d'Orgevals lunch "al fresco" at a massive stone table in the garden. For intimate dinners indoors they relocate to a rustic wooden table in the living room set with wrought-iron chairs.*

RIGHT: *A Louis XIII four-poster bed, decorated with plumes, occupies a place of honour in the living room. The room is, in fact, multifunctional, being a place where Jean and Dorothée can dine, sleep and entertain.*

VORHERGEHENDE DOPPELSEITE: *Ihre Mahlzeiten nehmen die d'Orgeval entweder am großen Steintisch im Garten oder im gemütlichen Wohnzimmer an einem rustikalen Tisch mit schmiedeeisernen Stühlen ein.*

RECHTS: *Das Wohnzimmer dominiert ein Louis-XIII-Himmelbett mit Federbuschaufsätzen. Der multifunktionale Raum dient Jean und Dorothée als Schlaf-, Ess- und Empfangszimmer zugleich.*

DOUBLE PAGE PRECEDENTE: *Les d'Orgeval prennent leurs repas sur une grande table de pierre au jardin ou dînent en toute intimité dans le séjour sur une table rustique entourée de chaises en fer forgé.*

A DROITE: *Un lit à baldaquin d'époque Louis XIII garni de panaches trône dans le séjour. La salle est multifonctionnelle, car c'est ici que Jean et Dorothée dorment, dînent et reçoivent leurs amis.*

PREVIOUS PAGES: *An alcove in the living room doubles as a display cabinet, exhibiting the d'Orgevals' impressive collection of Provençal pottery from the 18th and 19th centuries.*
RIGHT: *Snuggle up in the heart of Roussillon in this magnificent four-poster bed hung with ochre-coloured drapes whose colour is picked up on the matching quilt. The 'prie-dieu' beside the bed is a fine example of 18th-century cabinet-making.*

VORHERGEHENDE DOPPELSEITE: *In einer Wohnzimmernische fand die ansehnliche Sammlung provençalischer Fayencen aus dem 18. und 19. Jahrhundert ihren Platz.*
RECHTS: *Es ist herrlich, in Roussillon unter einem ockerfarbenen Betthimmel und einem gleichfarbigen Steppbett aufzuwachen. Das Betpult links stammt aus dem 18. Jahrhundert.*

DOUBLE PAGE PRECEDENTE: *Dans une niche du séjour, les d'Orgeval ont trouvé l'endroit idéal pour exposer leur belle collection de faïences provençales du 18ᵉ et du 19ᵉ siècle.*
A DROITE: *Il fait bon se réveiller au cœur du Roussillon dans un lit à baldaquin drapé d'un tissu ocre recouvert d'un « piqué » de la même couleur. Le prie-Dieu à gauche est d'époque 18ᵉ.*

$\mathcal{L}$A GRANDE BEGUDE

Juliette & François Lochon

Goult

There are some magical places in this world which merely need to be woken from their slumbers. La Grande Bégude is one of these. The old coach inn, built in 1622, lies deep in the heart of the Lubéron, near an ancient Roman road, in the midst of picturesque countryside irrigated by the river Calavon. One day, a couple of wayfarers crossed its courtyard and mounted the ancient stone staircase. It would take all the audacity of photoreporter François Lochon and his partner Juliette's passion for décor to efface the ravages wreaked by time and the elements. The couple say the restoration process appeared interminably long as they strove to maintain the building's soul and preserve the original patina of its stonework and the sobriety of its architecture. The giant plane tree in the garden must certainly recall the Lochons' relentless onslaught and the multitude of local craftsmen who lent their skills day after day. The result is a magnificent guest house which exudes the warmth of a Provençal summer's afternoon and offers guests the charm of ancient beams, vaulted ceilings, antique furniture, romantic bathrooms and wonderfully big comfy beds. It looks as if La Grande Bégude has finally rediscovered its vocation.

LEFT: *The old coaching inn is secluded behind a high stone wall, which protects guests' privacy.*
PAGES 62–63: *Provence wouldn't be Provence without sweeping views across a lavender field. La Grande Bégude has its own heavenly blue vista.*

LINKS: *Eine hohe Mauer umgibt die einstige Poststation und schützt die Gäste vor aufdringlichen Blicken.*
SEITE 62–63: *Lavendelfelder sind fester Bestandteil der provençalischen Landschaft. Auch La Grande Bégude bildet da keine Ausnahme.*

A GAUCHE: *Un haut mur entoure l'ancien relais de poste et protège les hôtes des regards indiscrets.*
PAGES 62–63: *On ne peut s'imaginer la Provence sans la vue d'un champ de lavande. La Grande Bégude ne pouvait faire exception à la règle.*

Es gibt Orte, die geradezu danach „schreien", wachgeküsst zu werden. Dazu gehörte wohl auch die alte Poststation La Grande Bégude. Sie entstand 1622 an einer alten Römerstraße im Herzen des Lubéron, einer Landschaft, die dem Fluss Calavon ihre Fruchtbarkeit verdankt. Als eines Tages ein Ehepaar die Schwelle des Hauses überschritt, quer über den Hof ging und die weite, hellgelbe Steintreppe hinaufstieg, war es soweit. Ein forscher Reporter und seine Frau mit einem Faible für Dekoration machten sich daran, alle Spuren von Alter und Verwitterung zu tilgen. Juliette und François Lochon erinnern sich gut an die endlose Restaurierung: ihre Sorge, ob sie die Seele des Hauses, seine heimelige Stimmung, die Patina seines Steins und die schlichte Bauweise würden retten können. Auch die große Platane erinnert sich sicher an den zähen Kampf und die zahllosen Handwerker, die sich in einem fort die Klinke in die Hand gaben. Die Mühe hat sich gelohnt: Das Gasthaus verströmt den warmherzigen Charme eines Sommertags in der Provence und bezaubert mit seinen mächtigen Balken, den Deckengewölben, Stilmöbeln, romantischen Bädern und kuscheligen Betten. Die alte Poststation hat ihre wahre Berufung gefunden.

The swimming pool near the old coaching inn is surrounded by trees, shrubbery and lavender bushes.

Das Schwimmbecken liegt in der Nähe der alten Poststation inmitten von Bäumen, Sträuchern und Lavendel.

La piscine, située à proximité de l'ancien relais, est entourée d'arbres, d'arbustes et de lavande.

Il est des lieux qui attendent d'être libérés de leur profond sommeil. La Grande Bégude, un ancien relais de poste construit en 1622, situé au cœur du Lubéron près d'une ancienne voie romaine au milieu d'une campagne irriguée par la source du Calavon, en fait partie. Un jour, un couple a franchi le seuil, traversé la cour et gravi le grand escalier en pierre blonde. Il fallait un photoreporter audacieux et sa compagne passionnée par la décoration pour lutter contre les effets de l'âge et les ravages dus aux éléments. Juliette et François Lochon se souviennent d'une restauration qui leur a semblé interminable. Ils racontent leur souci de préserver l'âme de la maison, son ambiance accueillante, la patine de sa pierre et la sobriété de son architecture. Le grand platane se souvient sans doute de leur lutte acharnée et du passage d'une multitude d'artisans pour créer une maison d'hôtes chaude comme une fin de journée d'été provençal. La demeure offre le charme de ses poutres anciennes, de ses plafonds voûtés, de ses meubles classiques, de ses salles de bains romantiques et de ses grands lits douillets. L'ancien relais de poste a retrouvé sa vocation.

On the first floor landing, the austere architecture is broken by two simple decorative details: a garden bench and an old-fashioned rocking horse.

Auf dem Treppenabsatz im ersten Stock beleben nur eine Gartenbank und ein Schaukelpferd die ansonsten völlig schmucklose Architektur.

Sur le palier du premier étage, un banc de jardin et un cheval à bascule sont la seule note décorative dans cette architecture austère.

PREVIOUS PAGES: *In summer, La Grande Bégude resembles an earthly paradise where afternoons are spent lounging in a hammock in the cool shade provided by the fruit trees and olive trees.*
RIGHT: *The old plane tree, which has stood in the middle of the courtyard for over a century, spreads its branches above a long banquet table where guests gather to share a pastis aperitif, a meal or a simple chat.*

VORHERGEHENDE DOPPELSEITE: *Im Sommer verwandelt sich La Grande Bégude in ein Schlaraffenland. Es tut gut, den Tag in einer Hängematte unter schattigen Olivenbäumen zu verträumen.*
RECHTS: *Unter der alten Platane, die seit über hundert Jahren mitten im Hof steht, treffen sich die Gäste am langen Tisch zu einer Mahlzeit, einem Gläschen Pastis oder einfach einem gemütlichen Schwatz.*

DOUBLE PAGE PRECEDENTE: *L'été, La Grande Bégude se transforme en pays de Cocagne où il fait bon paresser dans un hamac à l'ombre des arbres fruitiers et des oliviers.*
A DROITE: *Sous le vieux platane qui se dresse depuis plus d'un siècle au milieu de la cour, les hôtes peuvent se réunir autour d'une longue table, le temps d'un repas, d'un verre de pastis ou d'un papotage convivial.*

PREVIOUS PAGES:
A refined and peaceful atmosphere reigns beneath the vaulted ceiling of the vast living room, where wing chairs and period furniture are silhouetted in sunlight filtering through the tall curtains.
RIGHT: *In this ballroom-sized suite on the first floor, a set of imposing wooden beams provide a loft canopy for the rococo bed. Furniture is kept to a minimum in the bedroom to emphasise the beauty of the room's volumes.*

VORHERGEHENDE DOPPELSEITE: *Unter der Gewölbedecke des Salons schufen die Eigentümer ein behagliches Ambiente. Durch die Vorhänge gedämpft, umschmeichelt das Sonnenlicht die bequemen Polstersessel und das klassische Mobiliar.*
RECHTS: *ein offener Dachstuhl als Baldachin über dem Rokoko-Bett. Das Schlafzimmer im ersten Stock ist groß wie ein Ballsaal, jedoch nur sparsam möbliert, um den Raum an sich zur Geltung zu bringen.*

DOUBLE PAGE PRECEDENTE: *Sous les voûtes du vaste salon, les propriétaires ont créé une ambiance feutrée. Les rideaux filtrent le soleil et la lumière sculpte la silhouette des bergères et du mobilier aux lignes classiques.*
A DROITE: *Une charpente imposante sert de baldaquin à un lit rococo dans une suite à l'étage. Grande comme une salle de bal, la chambre à coucher a été meublée sobrement pour mettre en valeur la beauté du volume.*

$\mathcal{U}$NE MAISON TROGLODYTE

Ménerbes

Provence is full of picturesque villages, perched atop rocky hill-sides, which add their singular beauty to the overall charm of the region. Ménerbes is one of these magical spots which, in the past, has drawn famous figures such as Dora Maar and Nicolas de Staël, and continues to attract artists and lovers of old stone. One day a French antique dealer roamed Ménerbes's labyrinthine streets and alleyways, lined with small Provençal houses and sumptuous residences, but decided to make his home in a troglo-dyte dwelling, partially built into the rockface. The house, made up of a multitude of tiny rooms whose forms curve up the steep incline of the hill, has a magnificent vaulted living-room carved directly into the rock which provides a cool and refreshing refuge in the summer months. Impressed by this truly unique setting, the new owner has transformed the stun-ning troglodyte dwelling into a backdrop for his vast collection of religious antiques. Set off by typical Provençal colours and period furniture, statues of Christ and the Virgin rub shoulders with angels and an amazing assortment of crucifixes, accentu-ating the charm and old-fashioned beauty of this exceptional spot.

ABOVE: *A cross, for-merly used in religious processions, is silhouet-ted against the bedroom window.*
LEFT: *A collection of religious objects assem-bled on a window sill makes a dramatic still life.*

OBEN: *Vor dem Schlaf-zimmerfenster zeichnet sich die Silhouette eines Prozessionskreuzes ab.*
LINKS: *Auf der Fens-terbank wurde ein Stillleben aus sakralen Objekten arrangiert.*

CI-DESSUS: *La sil-houette d'une croix de procession se profile contre la fenêtre de la chambre.*
A GAUCHE: *Sur l'ap-pui d'une fenêtre, une nature morte composée de quelques objets reli-gieux.*

Die Provence ist unglaublich reich an malerischen Dörfern, die wie i-Tüpfelchen über der wunderschönen Landschaft hoch oben auf felsigen Hängen thronen. Eines dieser bildhübschen Städtchen ist Ménerbes. Auf den Spuren berühmter Leute wie Dora Maar oder Nicolas de Staël fühlen sich Künstler und Liebhaber alter Gemäuer gleichermaßen angezogen von den märchenhaft verschlungenen Straßen und den von kleinen Häusern und stattlichen Palästen gesäumten Gassen. Ein ortsansässiger Antiquitätenhändler wählte als seinen Wohnsitz in Ménerbes eine Art Höhlenhaus, das teilweise in den Hang hineingebaut ist. Die Anordnung der zahlreichen kleinen Räume folgt genau der steil abfallenden Böschung. Unmittelbar in den Felsen geschlagen wurde ein überwölbter Raum, der auch in der Hitze des Sommers erfrischend kühl bleibt. Betört von dieser einzigartigen Konstellation beschloss der neue Besitzer, das Haus eigne sich ideal für seine umfangreiche Sammlung sakraler Objekte. Inmitten typisch provençalischer Farben und geschmackvoller alter Möbel bilden Madonnen, Christusstatuen, Engel und Kruzifixe unterschiedlicher Stile und Epochen ein ausgefallenes Ensemble von herrlich altmodischem Charme.

La Provence possède un véritable trésor de villages pittoresques, lesquels, perchés au sommet de collines rocheuses, semblent vouloir couronner ce magnifique pays de leur beauté singulière. Ménerbes ne fait pas exception à la règle et, suivant l'exemple de célébrités comme Dora Maar et Nicolas de Staël, des artistes et amateurs de vieilles pierres se sont sentis attirés par la magie de ses rues labyrinthiques et de ses ruelles bordées de petites maisons et de palais imposants. L'antiquaire qui s'est établi à Ménerbes a choisi une habitation troglodyte, construite partiellement dans le rocher. Composée d'une multitude de pièces aux dimensions modestes dont la disposition suit étroitement la pente raide de la colline, la maison possède une salle voûtée, creusée dans la masse rocheuse, qui peut servir de frais salon d'été. Séduit par cette demeure unique en son genre, notre antiquaire a décidé qu'elle servirait d'écrin à sa vaste collection d'objets religieux. Sur fond de couleurs provençales et soutenus par la présence de beaux meubles anciens, les Vierges, les Christ, les anges et les crucifix d'époques et de styles divers accentuent la beauté et le charme désuet de ce lieu hors du commun.

A 19th-century drape decorated with the image of a saint hangs in the stairway.

Im Treppenhaus hängt eine Kirchenfahne mit Heiligendarstellung aus dem 19. Jahrhundert.

Une bannière 19ᵉ ornée d'une image sainte a été accrochée dans la cage d'escalier.

FACING PAGE: *The cave is decorated with 18th-century furniture, antique benches and rustic stools. A collection of Provençal devotional objects adds a religious touch.*

ABOVE: *The master of the house is an avid collector of antique fabrics which came in handy for decorating the guestroom.*

RIGHT: *The vaulted grotto is a treasure trove of 18th-century antiques and rustic furniture. Visitors are always fascinated by the pink gravel floor.*

LINKE SEITE: *Das Gewölbe wurde ausgestattet mit Möbeln aus dem 18. Jahrhundert, rustikalen Bänken und Schemeln sowie einer Sammlung provençalischer Devotionalien.*

OBEN: *Als begeisterter Sammler alter Stoffe hatte der Hausherr keine Mühe, das Bett in diesem Gästezimmer stilvoll zu beziehen.*

RECHTS: *Das Höhlenhaus quillt über von Antiquitäten des 18. Jahrhunderts und rustikalen Möbeln. Der rosa Kiesboden verblüfft immer wieder Besucher.*

PAGE DE GAUCHE: *La grotte a été décorée avec un mobilier d'époque 18ᵉ, des bancs, des tabourets rustiques et une collection d'objets de piété provençaux.*

CI-DESSUS: *Grand collectionneur de tissus anciens, le maître de maison n'a pas eu à faire trop d'efforts pour habiller le lit dans une chambre d'amis.*

A DROITE: *La grotte voûtée foisonne d'antiquités 18ᵉ et de meubles rustiques. Son sol en gravier rose ne manque pas de surprendre les visiteurs.*

Jas de l'Ange

Eric & Laurence Hannoun

Orgon

A few years ago on this spot, there was nothing but a vast pine forest and the ruins of an old silkworm farm where scrub and undergrowth had grown wild. Eric and Laurence Hannoun, a Parisian couple with a passion for the south of France, were not to be put off, however. The Hannouns were intent on finding their own sun-filled corner of Provence and building the house of their dreams. With the help of architect Hugues Bosc and the finest craftsmen in the region, the couple set about building their home using the farm's original stonework. Showing extra-ordinary courage and tenacity in the face of technical difficul-ties such as levelling the ground, the Hannouns supervised the long and meticulous construction of their 'mas' (Provençal farmhouse). Their old-world-style abode is full of rustic charm with its blue shutters, trailing roses, quaint vegetable patch and its magnificent garden filled with olive trees and the heady scent of lavender. Eric and Laurence have now opened Jas de l'Ange as a guest house, inviting visitors to share the comfort and tran-quillity of their idyll, where exotic touches such as a Mauritanian tent blend perfectly with the spirit of Provence.

LEFT: *A ginger cat enjoys a siesta on an old garden bench near the terrace.*

LINKS: *Auf einer alten Bank an der Terrasse schläft eine rotweiße Katze den Schlaf der Gerechten.*

A GAUCHE: *Sur un vieux banc, près de la terrasse, un chat roux dort du sommeil des innocents.*

Hier fanden Eric und Laurence Hannoun einst nur einen großen Pinienhain und die überwucherten Ruinen einer alten Seidenraupenzucht. Doch davon ließen sich die beiden keineswegs
abschrecken. Schon seit langem suchten die gebürtigen Pariser
in ihrer geliebten Provence nach einem sonnigen Plätzchen für
ihr künftiges Traumhaus. Aus den Resten der verfallenen „magnanerie" erbauten sie es nun mit Hilfe des Architekten Hugues
Bosc und der geschicktesten Handwerker der Region. Mit Mut
und Beharrlichkeit meisterten die Hannouns alle Probleme von
der Nivellierung des Terrains bis zum langwierigen Bau selbst.
Dank ihrer archäologischen Liebe zum Detail entstand mit
dem Jas de l'Ange ein stilechtes provençalisches „mas" von fas-
zinierendem Charme. Das Haus mit seinen blauen Fensterläden und Kletterrosen, dem umfriedeten Küchengarten und
dem Park mit seinen Olivenbäumen, in dem es so herrlich nach
Lavendel duftet, wurde schon bald ein Gasthaus im besten
Sinne: Gemeinsam mit Eric und Laurence genießen die Besucher den Komfort und die ruhige Lage des Hauses. Exotische
Accessoires wie das mauretanische Zelt bilden die perfekte Er-
gänzung zum markanten Charme der Provence.

A l'origine, il n'y avait qu'une vaste pinède et les ruines d'une
ancienne magnanerie envahie par les broussailles. Mais il en
fallait bien plus pour décourager Eric et Laurence Hannoun,
Parisiens d'origine et amoureux du Midi, depuis toujours à la
recherche d'un coin de Provence ensoleillé et de la maison de
leurs rêves. Cette maison, ils la construisirent en utilisant les
pierres de la magnanerie, avec l'aide de l'architecte Hugues
Bosc et des meilleurs artisans de la région. Ce qui étonne aujourd'hui, c'est le courage et la ténacité des Hannoun qui ont
été confrontés à une montagne de difficultés comme le nivelle-
ment du sol et la construction lente et méticuleuse du « mas »,
exécutée avec une patience d'archéologue, pour aboutir à la
création d'une bâtisse trompeusement ancienne au charme fou.
Baptisée Jas de l'Ange, la maison rustique aux volets bleus, do-
tée de rosiers grimpants, d'un potager clos et d'un jardin ouvert
planté d'oliviers et qui embaume la lavande devint bientôt maison d'hôtes. Eric et Laurence partagent avec leurs hôtes le confort et le silence des lieux, une surprenante tente mauritanienne
et de petites touches exotiques qui se marient à merveille avec
l'âme de la Provence.

The owners have erected
a Mauritanian tent in
the courtyard, adding
an exotic note to their
typically Provençal
dwelling.

*Vor dem typisch proven-
çalischen Haus errich-
teten die Besitzer ein
mauretanisches Zelt,
dessen Fremdheit in die-
sem Umfeld ins Auge
sticht.*

*Devant la maison typi-
quement provençale, les
propriétaires ont dressé
une tente mauritanien-
ne. Le dépaysement est
garanti cent pour cent !*

ABOVE: *Secluded behind high stone walls and shaded by overhanging greenery, the terrace makes an ideal spot for al fresco dining.*
RIGHT: *Provençal flavours mingle with North African spices beneath the tapering lid of a tajine.*
FACING PAGE: *A colourful lounge area behind the main door welcomes guests from around the world. The lanterns bathe the setting in magical Oriental light by night.*

OBEN: *Mit ihren hohen Mauern und der schattigen Pergola, die sich darüberspannt, ist die Terrasse ein ideales Plätzchen für Mahlzeiten im Freien.*
RECHTS: *Wer sagt, ein Tajine könne die Gewürze Afrikas nicht mit den Aromen der Provence paaren?*
RECHTE SEITE: *Nahe der Eingangstür lädt eine gemütliche Ecke Gäste aus der ganzen Welt zum Verweilen ein. Laternen verströmen ein geheimnisvoll orientalisches Licht.*

CI-DESSUS: *La terrasse, entourée de hauts murs et ombragée par une tonnelle, est le lieu rêvé pour des repas à la fraîche.*
A DROITE: *Qui prétend que les saveurs de Provence et les épices africaines ne peuvent cohabiter dans la tajine ?*
PAGE DE DROITE: *Près de la porte d'entrée un coin repos accueille les hôtes venus du monde entier. Les lanternes évoquent les soirées magiques teintées d'Orient.*

LEFT: *The Maurita-nian tent is a riot of colour and decorative motifs. An exotic spot for a siesta or for a drink after a long hard day lounging by the pool.*
FACING PAGE: *A romantic lacquered white bed, an elegant canopy of fine gauze curtains set off against pale lemon walls: three perfect reasons to linger at the Jas de l'Ange.*

LINKS: *Das maure-tanische Zelt leuchtet weithin mit seinen bunten Dekorationen. Ein idealer Platz für eine Siesta oder zum Abschluss eines langen, faulen Tages am Pool.*
RECHTE SEITE: *Ein Baldachin aus durch-scheinenden Vorhängen, ein weiß lackiertes ro-mantisches Bett und zitronengelbe Wände – drei gute Gründe für ein paar Tage im Jas de l'Ange.*

A GAUCHE: *La tente mauritanienne brille de toutes ses décorations bariolées. C'est l'endroit idéal pour faire la sieste et pour terminer une longue journée passée au bord de la piscine.*
PAGE DE DROITE: *Un baldaquin drapé de rideaux diaphanes, un lit romantique laqué blanc et des murs jaune citron : trois raisons pour passer quelques jours au Jas de l'Ange.*

RIGHT: *A lacquered yellow wardrobe stands against a backdrop of vibrant yellow walls. A geranium-red lampshade picks up a vermilion stripe on the bedcover. The Midi sun appears to have stimulated the decorators, inspiring them to use a bold colour scheme.*
FOLLOWING PAGES: *A wrought-iron bed stands in the shade of a tree, the mosquito net draped from an overhanging branch flapping in the gusts of the Mistral.*

RECHTS: *Ein knallgelb lackierter Schrank, leuchtend gelbe Wände und ein Lampenschirm im Geranienrot der Streifen der Tagesdecke: Die südfranzösische Sonne muss den Innenausstatter zu solch kühnen Nuancen inspiriert haben.*
FOLGENDE DOPPELSEITE: *Ein schmiedeeisernes Bett im Schatten von Bäumen. Das Moskitonetz hängt von einem Ast herab und bläht sich unter den Böen des Mistral.*

A DROITE: *L'armoire laquée jaune vif, les murs d'un jaune vibrant et l'abat-jour qui fait écho au rouge géranium du couvre-lit rayé prouvent que le soleil du Midi a stimulé la palette des décorateurs et leur a inspiré une gamme audacieuse.*
DOUBLE PAGE SUIVANTE: *Un lit en fer forgé à l'ombre d'un arbre. La moustiquaire accrochée à l'une des branches se bat contre les bourrasques du Mistral.*

L A   M A I S O N   R O Q U E

Gérard Drouillet

Eygalières

Gérard Drouillet must often have had his striking features likened to those of a Roman emperor. And he has doubtless heard countless times that his violent and poetic paintings possess a powerful inner force. Drouillet prefers to stand quietly at his easel, letting his work speak for itself. Born in Marseilles after the war and greatly influenced by the fact he grew up by the sea, Drouillet went on to carve out a reputation as a promising artist. And then he met the antique dealer Bernard Paul and laid aside his brushes for a time, joining Paul in his quest for the rare and perfect object. Paul, a gentle and highly cultivated man, was gifted with an exceptional eye. Having lived in Alsace, he made his home in the Lubéron where he did much to contribute to the popularity of L'Isle-sur-la-Sorgue, opening the famous Espace Béchard. Following Paul's tragic death in 2000, Gérard decided to stay on in the Maison Roque, a robust 16th-century residence which once housed a silkworm farm. In collaboration with his partner, Frédéric Gigue, Drouillet has kept Bernard Paul's memory alive, filling the interiors of the Maison Roque with furniture, artwork and major pieces of 20th-century design. The walls are also hung with his own intriguing paintings.

LEFT: *Working in his tall, light-filled studio, Gérard Drouillet has just put the finishing touch to an abstract triptych.*

LINKS: *In dem hohen, lichterfüllten Atelier steht ein gerade fertig gewordenes Triptychon von Gérard Drouillet.*

A GAUCHE: *Dans son atelier haut et clair Gérard Drouillet vient de terminer un tableau en forme de triptyque.*

Dass er den Charakterkopf eines römischen Kaisers besitzt, hat er sicher schon oft gehört. Ebenso oft spricht man von der bemerkenswerten inneren Kraft seiner Gemälde und ihrer ebenso poetischen wie brutalen Symbolik. Gérard Drouillet lässt seine Bilder für sich sprechen. In der Nachkriegszeit in Marseille geboren und geprägt von mediterraner Gelassenheit, machte er sich als Maler schon früh einen Namen. Als er Bernard Paul kennen lernte, ließ er Pinsel und Palette eine Zeit lang ruhen, um gemeinsam mit dem Antiquitätenhändler nach dem Schönen und Ausgefallenen zu suchen. Paul besaß eine sanfte, kultivierte Art und einen sicheren Blick für das Außergewöhnliche. Von seiner elsässischen Heimat zog es ihn ins Lubéron, wo er mit dem Espace Béchard einen maßgeblichen Beitrag zur Popularität der L'Isle-sur-la-Sorgue leistete. Nach Bernards tragischem Tod im Jahr 2000 blieb Gérard in La Maison Roque wohnen, einem massiven Bau aus dem 16. Jahrhundert, einst eine Seidenraupenzucht. Gemeinsam mit seinem Partner Frédéric Gigue hält er dort das Andenken an Bernard Paul wach mit exquisiten Möbeln und Bildern, herausragenden Designobjekten des 20. Jahrhunderts und seinen eigenen fesselnden Gemälden.

The simple graphic lines of designer furniture and the harmony of form and volume turn every corner into a subtle collage.

Nüchtern-geradlinige Designermöbel, Harmonie zwischen Raum und Formen, jede Ecke dieses Hauses ist subtil komponiert.

Graphisme sobre des meubles design, harmonie entre formes et volumes, chaque coin de la maison dénote un assemblage subtil.

Il a une belle tête d'empereur romain, on a déjà dû le lui dire souvent. Comme on a dû lui répéter que sa peinture traduit une force intérieure remarquable et que ses symboles sont à la fois violents et poétiques. Pensif devant son chevalet, Gérard Drouillet laisse parler ses œuvres. Né à Marseille après la guerre, marqué par la douceur de vivre « en fond de mer », il s'est taillé une carrière de peintre prometteuse. Et puis il a rencontré l'antiquaire Bernard Paul et rangé un temps ses pinceaux pour se joindre à lui dans sa recherche continuelle du beau et du rare. Paul, un homme doux et cultivé, était doté d'un œil exceptionnel pour l'objet exceptionnel. Après avoir vécu en Alsace, il s'était installé dans le Lubéron où il contribua largement à l'immense popularité de l'Isle-sur-la-Sorgue en y créant l'Espace Béchard. Après la disparition tragique de Bernard en 2000, Gérard a décidé de rester à la maison Roque, une robuste bâtisse du 16e siècle qui abrita jadis une magnanerie. Avec son partenaire Frédéric Gigue, Drouillet continue à honorer la mémoire de Paul en s'entourant de meubles et de tableaux de qualité, de pièces majeures du design du 20e siècle et de tableaux fascinants qui portent sa signature.

Drouillet's paintings sit perfectly with vintage furniture from the 1960s and 70s.

Drouillets Gemälde harmonieren vorzüglich mit den Möbeln aus den 1960er und 70er Jahren.

Les tableaux de Drouillet se marient avec bonheur aux meubles vintage des années 1960 et 70.

LEFT: *Immaculate white walls dominate in the bathroom. A black-lacquered straw-bottomed chair, a veritable gem of 1950s design, is elegantly silhouetted against a stark white wall.*

FACING PAGE: *In a corner of his studio, the artist has set up a simple worktable where a portrait of Picasso sits in permanent residence.*

LINKS: *Im Bad dominiert makelloses Weiß, doch vor einer glatten, schmucklosen Wand hebt sich die zierliche Silhouette eines schwarzen Stuhles mit Geflecht aus den 1950er Jahren elegant ab.*

RECHTE SEITE: *In einer Ecke des Ateliers hat der Maler einen sehr schlichten Arbeitstisch aufgestellt, auf dem eine Fotografie von Picasso ihren Platz hat.*

A GAUCHE: *Dominée par un blanc immaculé, la salle de bains abrite néanmoins une chaise 1950 paillée et laquée noir dont la silhouette frêle et élégante se détache sur un pan de mur dépouillé.*

PAGE DE DROITE: *Dans un coin de l'atelier, l'artiste a installé une table de travail d'une sobriété remarquable sur laquelle trône en permanence le portrait de Picasso.*

LEFT: *In the living room, Drouillet proves the truth of the Oscar Wilde maxim that "all beautiful things belong to the same age." A group of African statuettes and pieces of 1950s pottery are juxtaposed with a 40s baroque chair, an elegant lamp and a 50s sideboard.*
FACING PAGE: *Gérard is sensitive to the allure of minimalism. The dining room bears no trace of ostentation.*

LINKS: *Im Wohnraum belegt Drouillet Oscar Wildes Maxime: „Alle schönen Dinge gehören der selben Zeit an." Die afrikanischen Statuetten und die Keramiken aus den 1950ern vertragen sich gut mit Lampe und Anrichte aus derselben Zeit sowie dem „Barocksessel" aus den 40ern.*
RECHTE SEITE: *Gérard bevorzugt schnörkellose Linien, im Esszimmer regiert edle Schlichtheit.*

A GAUCHE: *Dans le séjour, Drouillet prouve la véracité de la maxime « toutes les belles choses appartiennent à la même époque », signée Oscar Wilde. Ici les statuettes africaines et des faïences « fifties » cohabitent paisiblement avec un siège 1940 baroque, une lampe et une armoire-buffet des années 50.*
PAGE DE DROITE: *Gérard est sensible au design épuré. Rien d'ostentatoire dans la salle à manger.*

LEFT: *Architecture plays a prominent role in this converted silk farm. Restoring the building's original beams and wooden floors, the owner has decorated the interior with designer furniture from the 1950s, a pair of 1900 vases, and a group of elegant desk-lamps.*

FACING PAGE: *Drouillet is passionate about wood, in all aspects and forms. Here, an Afric-an stool sits next to an 18th-century 'banquette' while, to the left, a De Stijl-inspired chair is juxtaposed with a rustic wooden table.*

LINKS: *In der einstigen Seidenraupenzucht spielt die Architektur die Hauptrolle. Die authentischen Holzdecken und -böden kombinierte der Hausherr mit Objekten der 1950er Jahre, Vasen um 1900 sowie einfachen Schreibtischlampen.*

RECHTE SEITE: *Drouillet liebt Holz in jeder Erscheinungsform: Hier sind es ein afrikanischer Schemel und eine Bank aus dem 18. Jahrhundert. Links ein an De Stijl orientierter Stuhl neben einem rustikalen Tisch.*

A GAUCHE: *Dans cette ancienne magnanerie, l'architecture joue un rôle majeur. Entre poutres et planchers d'époque, le maître de maison a juxtaposé des créations des années 1950, une paire de vases 1900 et des lampes de bureau anonymes.*

PAGE DE DROITE: *Drouillet aime le bois, quel que soit son aspect et sous toutes ses formes. Ici un tabouret africain côtoie une banquette 18ᵉ. A gauche, une chaise inspirée par De Stijl tient compagnie à une table rustique.*

Saint-Rémy-de-Provence

According to Jean Claude Brialy, a decade or so ago his beautiful Provençal abode was just an "ugly old gatekeeper's house." The renowned French actor and film director, one of the leading figures of the Nouvelle Vague, made his screen presence felt in Claude Chabrol's "The cousins." It was around this same period that Brialy first discovered Provence. The actor hesitated a little too long over his original project of buying an 'hôtel particulier' in Saint-Rémy-de-Provence, but he finally settled in the region in 1995, after sending his friend Bruno off to find "a home to retire to." Working in collaboration with the architect Hugues Bosc and landscape gardener Michel Semigny, Brialy's 1900-style house – an anonymous-looking villa surrounded by wasteland – was transformed into a stunning home filled with mementoes the actor has accumulated in the course of his career and his trips around the world. "I knew exactly what I wanted," says Brialy, "A big sun-filled kitchen painted Van Gogh yellow. A spacious Provençal living-room, a guestroom, a bedroom with a terrace and a pool which wouldn't look 'nouveau riche' but blended into the garden like a natural pond. I wanted a garden that would stay green all year round, a siena façade and a big orangery." Jean Claude and Bruno's home is all this and more!

The shutters of the
actor's bedroom open
out onto stunning
views of the garden.

Von seinem Schlaf-
zimmer aus schaut
Brialy in den herr-
lichen Garten.

De sa chambre le co-
médien a une vue
imprenable sur le jar-
din.

Vor rund zehn Jahren, erzählt Jean Claude Brialy, war sein schönes provençalisches Heim noch ein hässliches Schranken-wärterhäuschen. Als einer der Stars der Nouvelle Vague ist der Schauspieler und Regisseur auch heute noch ein Begriff, nicht zuletzt wegen seiner atemberaubenden Präsenz in Filmen wie „Schrei, wenn du kannst" von Claude Chabrol. In jener Zeit verliebte er sich in die Provence. Bei einem Stadthaus in Saint-Rémy-de-Provence zögerte er etwas zu lange, doch die zweite Chance kam 1995, als er seinen Freund Bruno auf die Suche nach einem „Altersruhesitz" schickte. Mit Hilfe des Architekten Hugues Bosc und des Landschaftsgärtners Michel Semigny verwandelte sich das Jahrhundertwende-Haus – ein anonymer Klotz mit Grundstück – in ein charmantes Domizil voller Erinnerungen. „Ich wusste genau, was ich wollte", erzählt Brialy: „Eine große, helle Küche in Van-Gogh-Gelb. Einen großen provençalischen Salon, ein Gästezimmer, ein Terrassenzimmer und einen Pool, der nicht neureich wirken sollte, sondern wie ein Gartenteich. Und natürlich einen immergrünen Garten, eine sienagelbe Fassade und eine große Orangerie." Für Jean Claude und Bruno wurde der Traum Wirklichkeit.

Si l'on en croit Jean Claude Brialy, sa belle maison provençale n'était il y a une dizaine d'années qu'une vilaine « maison de garde-barrière ». On revoit le célèbre acteur et réalisateur, figu-re de proue de la Nouvelle Vague, crevant l'écran dans « Les cousins » de Claude Chabrol. C'est à cette époque qu'il décou-vrit la Provence. Il hésita trop longtemps à acheter un hôtel par-ticulier à Saint-Rémy-de-Provence, mais il a eu sa revanche en 1995 après avoir demandé à son ami Bruno de partir à la recher-che d'une « maison de retraité ». Avec l'aide de l'architecte Hugues Bosc et du paysagiste Michel Semigny, la maison de style 1900 – un pavillon anonyme entouré d'un terrain vague – est devenue une demeure charmante qui abrite des souvenirs accumulés tout au long d'une brillante carrière et au fil de vo-yages à travers le monde. « Je savais ce que je voulais » raconte Brialy. « Une grande cuisine claire, jaune comme le jaune Van Gogh. Un grand salon provençal, une chambre d'amis, une chambre avec terrasse et une piscine qui ne ferait pas 'nouveau riche' mais ressemblerait à un bassin de jardin. Et puis un jar-din vert toute l'année, une façade jaune de Sienne et une grande orangerie ». Jean Claude et Bruno ont réalisé leur rêve.

Jean Claude Brialy dis-likes the electric blue of Californian swimming pools and has trans-formed his own into a natural stretch of water.

Jean Claude Brialy ver-abscheut die stahlblauen kalifornischen Pools. Sein eigenes Schwimm-becken wirkt wie ein natürlicher Teich.

Jean Claude Brialy ab-horre les piscines califor-niennes bleu électrique. Il a transformé la sienne en plan d'eau.

Working in collaboration with the architect and landscape gardener Michel Semigny, Jean Claude and Bruno have transformed a former wasteland in-to a luxuriant garden. An equally incredible metamorphosis has been effected on the house, which began life as a suburban bungalow but is now a magnificent Provençal villa.

Mit Hilfe des Landschaftsarchitekten Michel Semigny machten Jean Claude und Bruno aus einer Brachfläche einen bezaubernden Garten. Die gleiche Metamorphose durchlief auch das Gebäude, das seine Karriere als banales Wohnhaus begann und sich heute als bildschöne provençalische Villa präsentiert.

Avec l'aide de l'architecte-paysagiste Michel Semigny, Jean Claude et Bruno ont transformé un terrain vague en un jardin plein de charme. La métamorphose fait écho à celle de la maison qui commença sa carrière comme pavillon de banlieue et resplendit aujourd'hui de toute sa beauté de villa provençale.

LEFT: *White lacquered cane furniture and wrought-iron tables turn the terrace and its overhanging arbour into an elegant open-air dining room.*

FACING PAGE: *In Jean Claude's bedroom, 18th-century wood panelling in striking shades of absinthe reflect the intense southern light. Beyond the landing, a glimpse of Bruno's room furnished with a rustic four-poster bed.*

LINKS: *Weiße Rattanmöbel und schmiedeeiserne Tischchen machen die schattig belaubte Terrasse zu einem Freiluftsalon.*

RECHTE SEITE: *Die Wände in Jean Claudes Schlafzimmer sind mit leuchtend absinthgrünen Vertäfelungen aus dem 18. Jahrhundert bedeckt. Auf der anderen Flurseite erspäht man in Brunos Schlafzimmer das rustikale, weiß bezogene Himmelbett.*

A GAUCHE: *Des meubles en rotin laqué blanc et des tables en fer forgé transforment la terrasse et sa tonnelle en un salon de plein air.*

PAGE DE DROITE: *Dans la chambre de Jean Claude, des boiseries 18e couleur d'absinthe habillent les parois et captent la lumière. Au-delà du palier, on aperçoit la chambre de Bruno et son lit à baldaquin rustique habillé de blanc.*

LA MAISON DE FREDERIC MISTRAL

Maillane

"Now my young man, I've done my duty. You know far more than anyone ever taught me!" These were the words Frédéric Mistral's father imparted to his son on learning he had just earned his law degree. At the age of 21, Mistral took an even more momentous decision, vowing to "revive a sense of race in Provence and bring about a resurrection by restoring the historic mother tongue of my country and bringing Provençal back into fashion with the flame of divine poetry." The author of the Provençal language dictionary, "Lou Trésor dóu Felibrige," and the epic poem, "Mireille," was also renowned for founding Arles's famous museum of ethnography, the "Museon Arlaten." Mistral set up home in Maillane in 1876. "I'm currently surrounded by builders," he wrote to a friend, shortly afterwards, "I'm having a small but pleasantly comfortable house built in the garden you saw, looking out onto the Alpilles." In his last will and testament penned on 7 September 1907 the legendary poet left his property to the local commune, thus preserving his home for posterity. Mistral, whose motto was "Lou souléou me fai canta" – the sun makes me sing – may have passed away long ago, but his spirit still haunts this charming Provençal abode.

LEFT: *In the late 19th century, bourgeois tastes favoured the baroque.*
PAGES 108–109: *This house preserves the vestiges of a bygone era. Pushing back the ancient wooden door, visitors discover the comfortable circumstances of a well-to-do Provençal family.*

LINKS: *Ende des 19. Jahrhunderts liebte das Bürgertum barocke Formen.*
SEITE 108–109: *Das ganze Haus zeugt von der Lebensart vergangener Zeiten und gewährt uns einen kurzen Blick in die plüschige Behaglichkeit einer wohl situierten Familie.*

A GAUCHE: *A la fin du 19ᵉ siècle le goût bourgeois était aux formes baroques.*
PAGES 108–109: *Cette maison témoigne de l'art de vivre d'une certaine époque et nous fait entrer dans le monde quotidien et l'ambiance feutrée d'une famille aisée.*

„Und nun, mein lieber Junge, habe ich meine Pflicht erfüllt. Du weißt viel mehr, als ich einst lernte", sprach Vater Mistral, als sein Sohn das Jurastudium abschloss. Mit 21 Jahren nahm sich Frédéric vor, „in der Provence das Gefühl für die eigene Herkunft neu zu wecken, durch die Wiederbelebung der Muttersprache und Geschichte meines Landes eine Wiedergeburt herbeiführen und das Provençalische durch den Einfluss und die Flamme der göttlichen Poesie populär zu machen." Er schrieb das provençalische Wörterbuch „Lou Trésor dóu Felibrige", das herrliche Versepos „Mireille", gründete das „Museon Arlaten", das ethnographische Museum von Arles, und zog 1876 nach Maillane. „Ich bin derzeit von Maurern umgeben", schrieb er an einen Freund, „Ich lasse mir ein kleines, aber bequemes und hübsches Haus im Garten bauen, den Sie kennen, mit Blick auf die Alpilles." In seinem Testament vom 7. September 1907 vermachte der Dichter seinen Besitz der Gemeinde Maillane und sorgte so dafür, dass das Haus der Nachwelt erhalten blieb. „Lou souléou me fai canta" – die Sonne bringt mich zum Singen – war Mistrals Motto: In seinem schönen provençalischen Haus scheint seine Stimme heute noch lebendig zu sein.

This washstand, just off the main bedroom, is a picture of monastic simplicity.

Die Waschecke gleich neben dem Schlafzimmer besticht durch klösterliche Einfachheit.

Situé à côté de la chambre à coucher, le coin toilette étonne par son caractère monacal.

« Maintenant mon beau gars, moi j'ai fait mon devoir. Tu en sais beaucoup plus que ce qu'on m'a appris », dit le père de Frédéric Mistral à son fils qui venait d'obtenir sa licence de droit. A 21 ans, le jeune Mistral prend la résolution de « raviver en Provence le sentiment de race, provoquer une résurrection par la restauration de la langue maternelle et historique de mon pays, rendre la vogue au provençal par l'influx et la flamme de la divine poésie ». Auteur du « Trésor dóu Felibrige », un dictionnaire de la langue provençale, de l'inoubliable poème épique « Mireille », et créateur du célèbre musée ethnographique arlésien, le « Museon Arlaten », Mistral s'établit à Maillane en 1876. « Je suis actuellement au milieu des maçons – écrit-il à un ami – « Je me fais bâtir une maison petite mais commode et agréable, dans le jardin que vous connaissez, en face des Alpilles ». Dans son testament du 7 septembre 1907 le grand poète lègue sa propriété à la commune de Maillane, préservant ainsi sa maison pour la postérité. Celui qui avait pour devise « Lou souléou me fai canta » nous a quitté, mais son ombre rôde toujours dans cette belle demeure provençale.

The dining room is decorated with beautiful old Provençal furniture and local faïences.

Das Speisezimmer mit seinen schönen provençalischen Möbeln und Fayencen aus der Region.

La salle à manger abrite de beaux meubles provençaux et des faïences régionales.

L'HOTEL DE BOURNISSAC

Christian Tortu

Noves

The Hôtel de Bournissac is an austere-looking 17th-century mansion in Noves, a sleepy southern French town haunted by the ghosts of Laura and Petrarch. After centuries of pomp and splendour, the Bournissac fell into abandon and suffered years of neglect. But the mansion's new owner, Christian Tortu, has respected its venerable age and undertaken a renovation which has not altered the original patina of stone or woodwork. Nor has he touched the walls' flaking paintwork or stirred centuries of noble dust. Tortu is an artist, an inspired florist and creative arranger with a gift for bringing out the beauty in bouquets of twigs, rose-petal covered lampshades, or unusual organic arrangements which prove that fruit and vegetable matter are as much a part of his artistic vocabulary as flowers. Tortu has brought an artist's eye to his Noves home, preserving the Bournissac's beautiful Zuber wallpaper and its antique curtains and leaving the worn floorboards exactly as they are. These decorative touches bear witness to the passing fads and fashions the house has lived through in its history. This magical place, charged with genuine atmosphere, proves that one does not necessarily have to destroy the past to create new beauty.

LEFT: *All the period features of the house have been carefully preserved, even the decorative window latches and original windowpanes.*
PAGES 114–115: *Secluded behind impressively high stone walls, Christian Tortu's garden is a haven of peace and tranquillity.*

LINKS: *Das Haus konnte seine zeitgenössischen Details bewahren, bis hin zu den Drehriegeln und Butzenscheiben.*
SEITE 114–115: *Im Garten findet Christian Tortu Frieden und Stille hinter den beeindruckend hohen Mauern.*

A GAUCHE: *La maison a gardé tous ses détails d'époque, jusqu'aux espagnolettes et aux fenêtres à petits carreaux.*
PAGES 114–115: *Le jardin clos de murs d'une hauteur impressionnante offre à Christian Tortu la paix et le silence.*

Das Hôtel de Bournissac ist ein strenges Gebäude aus dem 17. Jahrhundert in Noves – diesem ruhigen Städtchen, das immer noch den Geist von Laura und Petrarca verströmt. Das Haus durchlebte glanzvolle Zeiten, wurde später vernachlässigt und verfiel zu guter Letzt. Der neue Besitzer Christian Tortu ist dennoch entschlossen, das hohe Alter des Hauses zu ehren: Patina, abblätternde Farbe und erlesener Staub bleiben unangetastet. Tortu ist Künstler, einfallsreicher Florist mit dem genialen Talent, Schönheit hervorzulocken: Ein Bündel Zweige, ein mit getrockneten Rosenblüten übersäter Lampenschirm oder ein ausgefallenes Arrangement mit Obst und Gemüse gehören ebenso zu seinem Repertoire wie Blumengebinde. In Tortus Haus in Noves werden die Zuber-Tapeten mit ihren atemberaubenden Panoramen noch ebenso in Ehren gehalten wie die alten Vorhänge, die wurmstichigen Dielen und jener Zierrat, der von all den Vorlieben und Modeerscheinungen zeugt, die dieses Haus kommen und gehen sah. Das Ergebnis? Tortu gelang es, einen magischen Ort, eine unvergessliche Atmosphäre herzustellen. Seine Art, Schönes zu schaffen ohne Bestehendes zu zerstören, dürfte einzigartig sein.

L'Hôtel de Bournissac, une sévère bâtisse datant du 17e siècle, est situé dans une rue de Noves – petite ville tranquille où rôdent les fantômes de Laure et de Pétrarque. Il a connu des siècles de faste et des années d'abandon et de négligence, mais son nouveau propriétaire Christian Tortu a décidé de respecter son âge vénérable et de ne point toucher à ses patines, à ses peintures écaillées et à sa poussière ennoblie par le temps. Tortu est un artiste, un fleuriste iconoclaste et un créateur inspiré qui a le don de mettre au jour la beauté d'un bouquet de branches, d'un abat-jour couvert de pétales de roses séchées ou d'une composition hors du commun qui prouve que les fruits et les légumes font autant partie de son vocabulaire artistique que les fleurs. Dans sa maison de Noves, Tortu s'est bien gardé de toucher aux papiers peints Zuber, des panoramiques d'une beauté impressionnante. Il a préservé pieusement les rideaux anciens, les planchers vermoulus et tout un ensemble d'éléments décoratifs qui témoignent des goûts et des modes que sa maison a vu défiler. Le résultat ? Un endroit magique. Une ambiance inoubliable. Et une démarche exemplaire qui prouve qu'on peut créer la beauté sans détruire.

LEFT: *In the entrance hall, a classical vase made of woven branches, designed by Tortu, sits on an antique sculptor's stand.*
FACING PAGE: *The dining room door opens onto a vista of antique panoramic wallpaper designed by Zuber.*
FOLLOWING PAGES: *Tortu came up with the innovative idea of leaving much of the house in its original state. Stone and wood patinas, floors and curtains, were left unchanged, as was Zuber's elegant wallpiece, "Les Indes," in the living room.*

LINKS: *Auf einem alten Bildhauerschemel im Eingangsbereich steht eine von Tortu gefertigte klassische Vase aus Zweigen.*
RECHTE SEITE: *Die Türen zum Speisesaal öffnen sich zwischen originalen Panorama-tapeten der renommierten Manufaktur Zuber.*
FOLGENDE SEITEN: *Als originelle Idee beließ Tortu einen großen Teil des Hauses im Original-zustand: Patina, Vertäfelungen, Böden und Vorhänge, im Wohnzimmer auch die Zuber-Tapete „Les Indes".*

A GAUCHE: *Dans l'entrée, un vase classique à base de branches signé Tortu a trouvé sa place sur une sellette de sculpteur ancienne.*
PAGE DE DROITE: *La porte de la salle à manger s'ouvre sur des parois décorées avec des papiers peints panoramiques d'époque signés Zuber.*
PAGES SUIVANTES: *Tortu a eu l'idée originale de laisser une grande partie de la maison en l'état : patines, boiseries, sols et rideaux et, dans le séjour, « Les Indes » imprimées par Zuber.*

LA BASTIDE

Au pied des Alpilles

"Decorators generally regale listeners with the classic restoration tale which starts out with a dilapidated old ruin that ends up miraculously transformed into a stunning new home. But in this case, things worked the other way round!" says interior decorator Lisa Keller, showing us round a superb 17th and 18th-century residence, situated in a picturesque village at the foot of the Alpilles. Lisa, who has harboured a long-term passion for Provence, is no stranger to such tales of metamorphosis. She has an extensive international clientele who swear by her experience and her expert eye for design. However, on this occasion she was somewhat taken aback when a client asked her to work contrary to her usual routine, transforming a house "in perfectly good condition" into a ruin (albeit a temporary one!) Plywood partitions, sliding glass doors and other "modern horrors" all had to go. The aim was to restore the magnificent Provençal 'bastide' to its original pale stone glory and 'hôtel particulier' luxury. In the process, Lisa managed to integrate antique furniture, period paintings and a superb collection of objets d'art which had been wasting away in storage. Decorator and client can rightfully claim Caesar's motto, "veni, vidi, vici," as their own!

ABOVE: *a marble statuette dating from 1925.*
PAGES 122–124: *Michel Semigny created a precise landscape design for the luxuriant garden, but the mistress of the house softened its strict lines with rose bushes.*

OBEN: *Marmorstatuette aus der Zeit um 1925.*
SEITE 122–124: *Für den herrlichen Garten zeichnete Michel Semigny einen strengen Entwurf, den die Dame des Hauses jedoch mit Rosenbüschen auflockerte.*

CI-DESSUS: *une statuette en marbre d'époque 1925.*
PAGES 122–124: *Michel Semigny a dessiné un plan rigoureux pour le magnifique jardin, mais la maîtresse de maison l'a adouci en plantant des rosiers.*

„Innenarchitekten erzählen sonst immer die gleichen Geschichten von abenteuerlichen Restaurierungen, die mit einem uralten, verfallenen Gemäuer beginnen und der wundersamen Verwandlung in ein Traumhaus enden. Bei diesem Haus war es genau andersherum", erzählt die Innenarchitektin Lisa Keller bei der Führung durch das herrliche Gebäude aus dem 17. und 18. Jahrhundert. Lisa Keller ist der Provence verfallen und solche Metamorphosen gewöhnt. Ihre internationale Kundschaft schätzt ihre Erfahrung und ihr stilsicheres Auge. Als eine Kundin von ihr verlangte, ein „wohlerhaltenes" Haus – vorübergehend – praktisch abzureißen, war sie zunächst leicht konsterniert. Doch es wäre unvorstellbar gewesen, all die „modernen" Scheußlichkeiten wie Wandpaneele oder gläserne Schiebetüren beizubehalten: Diese wunderbare „bastide" verdiente es, ihr ursprüngliches Flair zurückzuerlangen und wieder der noble Wohnsitz zu werden, der sie einst war. Eine Herausforderung war es auch, all die schönen alten Möbel, Gemälde und edlen Accessoires einzubeziehen, die in einem Lagerhaus auf ihr Comeback warteten. Cäsars Motto „veni, vidi, vici" dürfen Lisa und ihre Kundin nach dieser Arbeit wohl zu Recht reklamieren.

Romantic Belle Epoque style dominates in this guestroom where a 1900 beauty languishes beneath the bed's draped canopy.

Eines der Gästezimmer ist im Stil der Belle Epoque romantisch gestaltet. Unter dem Lambrequin lockt eine Schönheit von 1900.

Dans une chambre d'amis le ton est au romantisme Belle Epoque. Sous un baldaquin une beauté 1900 attire le regard.

« D'habitude les décorateurs vous racontent l'histoire classique d'une restauration rocambolesque qui commence avec une vieille maison en ruine et se termine par la transformation miraculeuse en une demeure splendide. Mais dans le cas de cette maison c'était bien le contraire », raconte la décoratrice Lisa Keller en faisant le tour guidé d'une splendide bâtisse datant du 17e et du 18e siècle située au cœur d'un charmant village au pied des Alpilles. Inconditionnelle de la Provence, Lisa Keller a pourtant l'habitude des métamorphoses. Sa clientèle internationale jure par son expérience et son œil averti. Mais quand sa cliente lui a demandé de transformer – temporairement – en ruine une maison « en bon état », elle a un peu tiqué. En fait, il était impensable de garder des murs en contreplaqué, des portes coulissantes en verre et autres horreurs « modernes ». Il fallait restituer à cette magnifique bastide sa blondeur d'antan et son côté « hôtel particulier » luxueux. Intégrer les beaux meubles anciens, les tableaux et une collection d'objets de qualité qui dormaient dans un garde-meuble était un autre défi. Lisa et sa cliente peuvent reprendre à leur compte le « veni, vidi, vici » de César et se reposer sur des lauriers bien mérités.

The elegant silhouette of the wrought-iron banister is accentuated by the simplicity of the monochrome staircase.

Das monochrome Treppenhaus lässt die elegante Silhouette des Geländers gut zur Geltung kommen.

La cage d'escalier monochrome met en valeur la silhouette élégante de la rampe en fer forgée.

PREVIOUS PAGES: *Life in the depths of Provence provides pleasure for all the senses. This mouth-watering 'pissaladière' is a veritable feast for the eyes!*
LEFT: *In the entrance hall, a pair of 19th-century candelabra decorate a carved stone table.*
FACING PAGE: *The mistress of the house's bedroom is infused with romantic tones. Lisa Keller has brought her interior decorating skills to bear, juxtaposing 19th-century cast-iron chairs and a gilt-framed mirror above the baroque fireplace.*

VORHERGEHENDE DOPPELSEITE: *Im Herzen der Provence lässt es sich gut leben. Die von der Köchin Maury gebackene Pissaladière sieht gut aus und schmeckt auch so.*
LINKS: *Zwei Kandelaber aus dem 19. Jahrhundert zieren einen großen Steintisch am Eingang.*
RECHTE SEITE: *Das romantische Schlafzimmer der Hausherrin. Lisa Keller kombinierte raffiniert gusseiserne Stühle aus dem 19. Jahrhundert mit einem goldgerahmten Spiegel über dem barock geschwungenen Kamin.*

DOUBLE PAGE PRECEDENTE: *La vie est douce au cœur de la Provence et la pissaladière préparée par la cuisinière Maury un régal pour les yeux.*
A GAUCHE: *Dans l'entrée, une paire de candélabres 19ᵉ agrémentent une grande table de pierre.*
PAGE DE DROITE: *la chambre romantique de la maîtresse de maison. La décoratrice Lisa Keller a su marier des chaises de jardin 19ᵉ en fonte, un miroir à cadre doré et une cheminée aux formes baroques.*

ABOVE: *A fin-de-siècle ambience reigns in the conservatory, just off the master bedroom. The room is furnished with an elegant chaise-longue, a painted dressing screen and wrought-iron plant-holders.*
RIGHT: *The opulent décor is complemented with trinkets and curios. Every available surface is covered with decorative objects of some kind.*
FACING PAGE: *The bath adds an ostentatious edge, proving that a bathroom can be decorative as well as practical.*

OBEN: *Im Wintergarten neben dem großen Schlafzimmer beschwören ein Diwan, zierliche Blumenständer und ein Paravent mit diversen Tier- und Pflanzenmotiven das Fin de Siècle herauf.*
RECHTS: *Prunk heißt immer auch Nippes. In diesem Raum ist jeder Tisch, jede Nische mit dekorativen Kleinigkeiten bestückt.*
RECHTE SEITE: *Die Badewanne zwischen Wandvertäfelungen im Directoire-Stil beweist, dass ein Bad nicht nur praktisch sondern auch repräsentativ sein kann.*

CI-DESSUS: *Ambiance fin de siècle pour la serre située près de la chambre maîtresse, grâce au lit de repos, aux jardinières et au paravent qui réunissent les éléments de la flore et de la faune.*
A DROITE: *Qui dit opulence dit aussi bibelots. Ici, les objets décoratifs envahissent chaque table et chaque guéridon.*
PAGE DE DROITE: *La baignoire entourée de boiseries dans le goût Directoire prouve que la salle de bains peut aussi devenir salon et chambre d'apparat.*

FACING PAGE: *Lisa Keller has installed an old stone sink under a side window, accentuating the simple, rustic feel of the kitchen.*
ABOVE: *The kitchen was converted in style, retaining many of its original features. Beams and flagstone floors give the room a rustic, romantic feel.*
RIGHT: *The mistress of the house loves to entertain and the names of all kinds of famous guests are chalked up on the quaint old slates above the stove.*

LINKE SEITE: *Unter dem kleinen Fenster ließ die Hausherrin eine alte Steinspüle einbauen, die den rustikalen Charakter der Küche unterstreicht.*
OBEN: *Die vorhandenen Elemente der Küche wurden belassen, um eine romantisch-rustikale Atmosphäre zu schaffen.*
RECHTS: *Die Hausherrin lädt gern Gäste zum Mittag- oder Abendessen ein. Die Schiefertafeln über dem Herd weisen illustre Namen auf.*

PAGE DE GAUCHE: *Près d'une petite fenêtre, la décoratrice a installé un évier en pierre ancien qui fait écho à l'aspect rustique de la cuisine.*
CI-DESSUS: *La cuisine a été aménagée en respectant les éléments anciens pour créer une ambiance à la fois rustique et romantique.*
A DROITE: *La maîtresse de maison adore recevoir à déjeuner et à dîner et ses ardoises, au-dessus du fourneau, sont remplies de noms célèbres.*

L'HOTEL PARTICULIER

Arles

Brigitte Pagès de Oliveira is not only a passionate advocate of Moroccan décor, she is also a great admirer of the Moroccan lifestyle and Moroccan values of courtesy and discretion. Four years ago, however, Brigitte installed herself not in Marrakech, but in the Midi where she bought the magnificent Hôtel de Chartrouse (the former abode of the Baron de Chartrouse who carried out excavations on the site of the old Roman theatre). Deciding to open the Chartrouse to the public as a hotel, Brigitte sought to transform the house into a stylish 'hôtel particulier.' Working in close collaboration with the architect Paul Anouilh, she dreamt up a décor scheme that did not revolve around reconstructing the original interiors. Guests will find no trace of 18th and 19th-century French splendours nor heavy Napoleon III-style tapestries. Instead, L'Hôtel Particulier features a subtle mix of classic antique furniture and Oriental touches which include colourful Moroccan lanterns hung around the pool, a garnet-red living-room decorated with exotic paintings, and charming light-filled bedrooms furnished with sumptuous poufs and four-poster beds worthy of a pasha's palace. Grisaille wallpaper and vases from the Far East complete this perfect fusion of styles and make L'Hôtel Particulier a haven of peace and beauty.

LEFT: *Rose petals float in an ornamental stone basin beside the pool, recalling the sumptuous "riyads" of Morocco.*

LINKS: *In der Stein-schale neben dem Schwimmbecken treiben Rosenblätter und erinnern an die zauberhaften „riyads" Marokkos.*

A GAUCHE: *Près de la piscine, une vasque en pierre dans laquelle flot-tent des pétales de roses évoque les magnifiques riyads du Maroc.*

Brigitte Pagès de Oliveiras Leidenschaft ist die Innenarchitektur und die Kunst zu leben – insbesondere die marokkanische Lebensart, an der sie die Gelassenheit, Höflichkeit und vor allem die zurückhaltende Art der Menschen schätzt. All das sind gute Gründe dafür, dass sie sich für die Hotellerie entschied und vor vier Jahren das Hôtel de Chartrouse kaufte. Einst residierte darin ein gleichnamiger Baron, der durch die Ausgrabung eines antiken Theaters zu Ruhm und Ehren kam. Mit Hilfe des Architekten Paul Anouilh verwandelte Brigitte das Haus in ein zauberhaftes „hôtel particulier", verzichtete jedoch darauf, auch das Interieur im Stil des 18. und 19. Jahrhunderts zu gestalten. Hier gibt es weder prunkvolle Kulissen für die Hofdamen von einst noch verstaubte Draperien, sondern eine subtile Komposition klassischer Möbel mit einem Hauch von Orient. Rings um das Schwimmbecken stehen marokkanische Leuchten, und im granatroten Salon hängen exotische Bilder; die hellen Zimmer beherbergen Himmelbetten und Sitzkissen wie aus tausendundeiner Nacht, Grisaille-Tapeten und fernöstliche Vasen – alles spiegelt Brigittes glückliche Hand für Stilgemische und macht das Hotel zu einem Ort des Friedens und der Schönheit.

The French windows of the living room silhouetted against a colourful floral carpet.

Die Glastüren des Salons werfen Schatten auf das hübsche Blumenmotiv des Teppichs.

Les portes-fenêtres du salon se dessinent sur un joli tapis à motif floral.

Brigitte Pagès de Oliveira a une véritable passion pour la décoration et l'art de vivre… au Maroc, pays dont elle apprécie la douceur de vivre, la courtoisie des habitants et leur discrétion. Voilà de bonnes raisons pour qu'elle s'éprenne de l'hôtellerie et qu'elle achète, il y a quatre ans, l'Hôtel de Chartrouse dans lequel habita jadis le baron de même nom, célèbre pour avoir dirigé les fouilles du théâtre antique. Transformant la maison en un charmant « hôtel particulier » avec l'aide de l'architecte Paul Anouilh, Brigitte n'a pas cherché à reconstruire les intérieurs d'époque 18e et 19e. Ici point de splendeurs dignes des belles marquises d'antan ni de lourdes tentures Napoléon III, mais un mélange subtil de meubles classiques conjugués à une touche d'orientalisme. Des lanternes marocaines autour de la piscine, un salon grenat orné de tableaux aux sujets exotiques et des chambres claires où cohabitent des lits à baldaquin, des poufs dignes du palais d'un pacha, des papiers peints style « grisaille » et des vases d'Extrême-Orient révèlent le goût de Brigitte pour le mariage des styles et font de L'Hôtel Particulier un havre de paix et de beauté.

White roses cascade from a 19th-century Médicis vase in the garden.

Gusseiserne Medici-Vase aus dem 19. Jahrhundert mit weißen Rosen im Garten.

Côté jardin, un vase Médicis 19e en fonte accueille des roses blanches.

RIGHT: *The raised pool in the garden lies in the shade of the house and is surrounded by elegant recliners, parasols and Moroccan lanterns.*
FOLLOWING PAGE: *Breakfast is served al fresco in the cool shade cast by the shutters of the French windows. The neighbouring water trough and fountain were once part of the old stables.*

RECHTS: *Das erhöhte Schwimmbecken liegt im Schatten des Hauses. Ringsum sind Sessel, Sonnenschirme und marokkanische Laternen verteilt.*
FOLGENDE DOPPEL-SEITE: *Im angenehm kühlen Schatten der Fensterläden vor den Terrassentüren ist der Frühstückstisch appetitlich gedeckt. Brunnen und Tränke stammen noch aus dem ehemaligen Pferdestall.*

A DROITE: *La piscine surélevée, située dans le jardin à l'ombre de la maison, est entourée de sièges, de parasols et de lanternes marocaines.*
DOUBLE PAGE SUIVANTE: *Fraîcheur et ombre garantis : au-delà des jalousies qui garnissent les portes-fenêtres on vient de dresser la table du petit-déjeuner. La fontaine et l'abreuvoir font partie des anciennes écuries.*

LEFT: *The morning room, decorated with aubergine-coloured walls, Orientalist paintings, baroque lamps and comfy club chairs, is a haven of peace and calm.*

FACING PAGE: *The rich vermilion tones of the dining room walls provide a striking contrast to the set of white-painted country chairs. The glass-fronted cabinet at the foot of the table showcases a superb collection of decorative pottery.*

LINKS: *Gemälde mit orientalischen Motiven, auberginefarbene Wände, barocke Leuchten und bequeme Clubsessel laden die Gäste im kleinen Salon zum Verweilen ein.*

RECHTE SEITE: *Im Speisezimmer bilden die leuchtend roten Wände einen schönen Kontrast zu den weiß gestrichenen Stühlen. Der Schrank an der Rückwand beherbergt eine Sammlung dekorativer Fayencen.*

A GAUCHE: *Peintures orientalistes, murs couleur aubergine, luminaires baroques et fauteuils-club confortables réjouissent les hôtes qui désirent s'attarder dans le petit salon.*

PAGE DE DROITE: *Dans la salle à manger, des murs rouge vif contrastent avec des chaises rustiques peintes en blanc. L'armoire au fond de la pièce abrite une collection de faïences décoratives.*

FACING PAGE: *18th-century wood panelling painted immaculate white makes the perfect backdrop for this elegant four-poster bed. The Oriental pink vase adds an agreeable touch of colour to the room.*
RIGHT: *A pair of terracotta lions, bearing ancient coats of arms, stand guard at the morning room door.*
FOLLOWING PAGES: *A pastoral grey-and-white camaieu adorns the wall of an upstairs bedroom, set off by white walls, white bed linen and a white Louis XV-style chair.*

LINKE SEITE: *Weiße Wandvertäfelungen aus dem 18. Jahrhundert bilden den Rahmen für das Himmelbett. Die Vase in Rosa bringt einen Hauch Farbe in den Raum.*
RECHTS: *Terrakotta-löwen mit Wappenschilden flankieren die Türen zum kleinen Salon.*
FOLGENDE DOPPELSEITE: *In einem der Schlafzimmer im ersten Stock hängt ein grauweißes Grisaille-Wandbild. Wände, Bettwäsche und Bezug des Louis-XV-Sessels sind reinweiß.*

PAGE DE GAUCHE: *Des boiseries 18ᵉ peintes en blanc sont l'arrière-plan idéal pour ce lit à baldaquin. Le vase oriental rose ajoute une note de couleur à la chambre.*
A DROITE: *Des lions en terre cuite portant des écussons se dressent de part et d'autre de la porte du petit salon.*
DOUBLE PAGE SUIVANTE: *Une des chambres à l'étage a été décorée d'un camaïeu de blanc et de gris. Les murs, la literie et le revêtement de la bergère style Louis XV sont blancs.*

GRAND HOTEL NORD-PINUS

Anne Igou

Arles

Napoleon III was a guest in number 10, a room later occupied by a host of other celebrities including Pablo Picasso and the toreador Luis Miguel Dominguín. The photographer Lucien Clergue stayed here on trips to Arles and it was here that Helmut Newton shot his memorable portrait of the actress Charlotte Rampling. Given the colourful history of the Grand Hôtel Nord-Pinus, Anne Igou was understandably keen to step into the shoes of the famous ex-proprietress Madame Germaine. The new owner set about breathing new life into the legendary hotel in 1989, after it had lain unoccupied for 15 years. "There was absolutely nothing of the original décor left," Anne recalls, "nothing but the two boat-shaped chandeliers and the console and baroque mirror in number 10. I had to start from scratch and restore everything!" Today's guests would find it hard to imagine such a colossal undertaking. The Spanish bullfighting posters, the photographs by Lucien Clergue and Peter Lindbergh, the retro furniture and the colours seem like they have always been there. With a statue of Mistral silhouetted against the hotel's name up in lights outside, Anne Igou can pride herself on having brought a legend back to life.

LEFT: *A statue of Frédéric Mistral stands proudly in the Place du Forum, observing the hustle and bustle of tourists trying to find a seat on the café terraces below.*

LINKS: *Das stolze Standbild Frédéric Mistrals dominiert die Place du Forum und schaut auf die Touristen herab, die sich auf den zahlreichen Caféterrassen tummeln.*

A GAUCHE: *La fière statue de Frédéric Mistral semble dominer la place du Forum et regarder les touristes qui essayent de trouver un siège à la terrasse d'un des nombreux cafés.*

Napoleon III. logierte in Zimmer 10, ebenso wie später Pablo Picasso, der Torero Luis Miguel Dominguín und viele andere Berühmtheiten. Zu den Gästen gehörten auch der Fotograf Lucien Clergue und Helmut Newton, der hier Charlotte Ramplings unsterbliches Porträt schuf. Als Anne Igou das Grand Hôtel Nord-Pinus in Arles übernahm, hatte sie deshalb allen Grund, das Werk im Geist der Vorbesitzerin Madame Germaine fortzusetzen. Nach 15 Jahren Dornröschenschlaf hauchte sie dem legendären Hotel 1989 neues Leben ein: „Vom alten Dekor war so gut wie nichts erhalten", erinnert sich Anne. „Lediglich die beiden schiffsförmigen Kronleuchter, das Konsoltischchen und der Barockspiegel in Zimmer 10 waren noch vorhanden. Alles musste ich erneuern, alles restaurieren!" Wer heute im Nord-Pinus absteigt, kann sich kaum noch vorstellen, was für eine Sisyphusarbeit dahintersteckt. Die spanischen Stierkampfplakate, die Farben, die Fotos von Lucien Clergue und Peter Lindbergh und das nostalgische Mobiliar wirken durch und durch original. Mag das Mistral-Denkmal vor der Tür dem Namensschild des Nord-Pinus auch den Rücken zukehren: Anne Igou weiß, was sie geschafft hat.

Napoléon III y occupa la chambre 10, précédant Pablo Picasso, le toréador Luis Miguel Dominguín et bien d'autres célébrités. Le photographe Lucien Clergue y a séjourné et Helmut Newton y a réalisé l'inoubliable portrait de l'actrice Charlotte Rampling. Anne Igou avait donc de bonnes raisons de reprendre le flambeau de la fameuse ex-directrice Madame Germaine en devenant à son tour propriétaire du Grand Hôtel Nord-Pinus à Arles. Elle a redonné vie en 1989 à cet endroit légendaire qui avait été inoccupé pendant 15 ans. « Il ne restait plus rien de l'ancien décor », se souvient Anne – « juste les deux lustres en forme de bateau et la console et le miroir baroque dans la 10. J'ai dû tout refaire. Tout restaurer ! » Aujourd'hui les hôtes du Nord-Pinus ne peuvent guère s'imaginer les travaux de Sisyphe qui ont été entrepris à l'époque. Les affiches de tauromachie espagnoles, les couleurs, les photographies de Lucien Clergue et de Peter Lindbergh et le mobilier rétro donnent l'impression d'avoir toujours été là. Dehors, la statue de Mistral semble tourner le dos à l'enseigne lumineuse du Nord-Pinus. Mais Anne Igou sait qu'elle a gagné le pari.

LEFT: *The monumental staircase is adorned with a Louis XV banister in elegant wrought iron and hung with antique posters.*
BOTTOM: *The convivial décor in the bar conjures up images of an old-fashioned bistrot from a Marcel Pagnol novel.*
FACING PAGE: *Anne Igou's rich red colour scheme makes a stunning backdrop for these photographs of famous bullfighters.*

LINKS: *das weitläufige Treppenhaus mit dem schmiedeeisernen Louis-XV-Geländer und alten Plakaten.*
UNTEN: *Die Dekoration der Bar erinnert an gemütliche Bistros wie bei Marcel Pagnol.*
RECHTE SEITE: *Für die Wände wählte Anne Igou Rot, das die schönen Fotos berühmter Stierkämpfer hervorhebt.*

A GAUCHE: *la vaste cage d'escalier avec sa rampe en fer forgé Louis XV et ses anciennes affiches.*
EN BAS: *La décoration du bar évoque l'ambiance conviviale des bistros à la Marcel Pagnol.*
PAGE DE DROITE: *Anne Igou a choisi des murs rouges pour exalter la beauté des photographies de toréadors célèbres.*

FOLLOWING PAGE: *Embroidered gauze curtains flutter in the summer breeze, bathing the restaurant in a soft glow.*
PAGE 153: *Many celebrities have slept in this magnificent upstairs bedroom.*
PAGES 154–155: *Napoleon III and Picasso both slept in the famous toreadors' suite. The baroque console and mirror made a stunning backdrop for Charlotte Rampling when she posed for photographer Helmut Newton.*

FOLGENDE SEITE: *Durchscheinende, bestickte Gardinen lassen sanftes Licht ins Restaurant und bewegen sich in der Sommerbrise.*
SEITE 153: *In diesem Bett in einem der Zimmer schliefen schon unzählige Berühmtheiten.*
SEITE 154–155: *Napoleon III. und Picasso übernachteten im „Torero-Zimmer". Barockkonsole und -spiegel dienten schon als Hintergrund für Helmut Newtons berühmtes Porträt von Charlotte Rampling.*

PAGE SUIVANTE: *Des rideaux diaphanes brodés tamisent la lumière qui baigne la salle de restaurant et flottent dans une brise d'été.*
PAGE 153: *Dans une chambre à l'étage, ce lit splendide a accueilli nombre de célébrités.*
PAGES 154–155: *Napoléon III et Picasso ont dormi dans la chambre des toréadors. La console et le miroir baroque ont aussi servi de décor à Charlotte Rampling quand elle a posé pour Helmut Newton.*

EMMANUEL DE SAUVEBŒUF

Nîmes

Many are those, over the centuries, who have succumbed to the timeless charm of Nîmes. It is not difficult to understand why Thomas Jefferson spent an entire day admiring the imposing architecture of the Maison Carrée. Nor why others, before and after the great statesman, have been seduced by the powerful combination of the southern French sun and the classic beauty of the town's ancient Roman relics. Antique dealer Emmanuel de Sauvebœuf is a man for whom beauty is a primordial consideration in life. So it was only natural he should build a house that makes the perfect backdrop for his superb collection of period furniture, paintings and objets d'art. De Sauvebœuf found his ideal setting in a quiet village just outside town. Visitors will be impressed by the house's austere façade and the absence of any superfluous ornamentation, and charmed by the typical Provençal garden. The antique dealer appears to have an innate talent for interior décor. He has created a skilful and harmonious mix of classical sculpture and antique furniture which stands as a tribute to French cabinet making. The ensemble is set off by a palette of agreeably subtle colours.

LEFT: *The kitchen cupboards are a veritable treasure trove of home-made jams and preserves.*

LINKS: *In den Küchenschränken stehen Gläser mit Eingemachtem und hausgemachter Konfitüre.*

A GAUCHE: *Les placards de la cuisine abritent des conserves et des confitures maison.*

Seit jeher lassen sich immer wieder Menschen vom Charme der Stadt Nîmes betören. Auch ohne allzu viel Fantasie versteht man, warum Thomas Jefferson sich einen ganzen Tag Zeit für die imposante Maison Carrée nahm oder warum andere vor und nach ihm dem perfekten Zusammenspiel von provençalischem Sonnenlicht und den Zeugen der römischen Antike verfallen sind. Für Menschen wie den Antiquitätenhändler Emmanuel de Sauvebœuf ist Schönheit oberstes Gebot. Da er alte Möbel, Gemälde und kostbare Dinge liebt und verkauft, ließ er sich ein Haus bauen, das für seine Schätze einen würdigen Rahmen bildet. Dieses entstand in einem ruhigen Dorf in der Nähe der Stadt. Die Besucher beeindruckt nicht nur der wunderschöne, typisch provençalische Garten, sondern auch das streng wirkende Haus, welches vollkommen frei von überflüssigem Zierrat ist. De Sauvebœuf besitzt ein angeborenes Talent für Innenarchitektur: Ihm gelingt einfach alles. Mit leichter Hand vereint er klassische Statuen und erlesene Stilmöbel, die den französischen Kunstschreinern zur Ehre gereichen, mit Porzellanfiguren und kostbarem Nippes. Das Ergebnis ist ein harmonisches, durch subtile Farben getragenes Ambiente.

Ils ont été nombreux au cours du temps à tomber sous le charme de Nîmes. Faut-il vraiment beaucoup d'imagination pour comprendre pourquoi Thomas Jefferson a passé toute une journée à contempler la silhouette imposante de la Maison Carrée ? Et pourquoi d'autres avant et après lui ont été séduits par la combinaison idéale du soleil de Provence et de la beauté classique des vestiges de l'Antiquité romaine ? L'antiquaire Emmanuel de Sauvebœuf est de ces hommes pour qui la beauté est une condition primaire. Il va de soi que cet amateur et marchand de meubles, de tableaux et d'objets de qualité a choisi de construire une maison digne de ses acquisitions. Il a créé la demeure qui lui convient dans un village calme, situé près de la ville. La maison fascine les visiteurs par son aspect sévère et dépouillé de tout ornement superflu ainsi que par son splendide jardin typiquement provençal. De Sauvebœuf peut se vanter également d'avoir un talent inné pour la décoration intérieure. Tout semble lui réussir. Avec une belle aisance, il a su marier harmonieusement une statuaire classique, de beaux meubles d'époque, qui font la gloire de l'ébénisterie française, et une palette de couleurs d'une subtilité remarquable.

RIGHT: *Could you ever have guessed that this magnificent Provençal house and garden were built just four years ago? A miracle, indeed!*
FOLLOWING PAGES: *Emmanuel de Sauve-bœuf has created a romantic garden filled with olive trees, a profusion of greenery and potted plants. An antique wooden birdcage daubed with blue paint is set off against drystone walls above an old garden table.*

RECHTS: *Dass dieses typisch provençalische Haus mit seinem Garten erst vor gerade einmal vier Jahren entstanden ist, ist kaum zu glauben.*
FOLGENDE DOPPEL-SEITE: *Olivenbäume und eine Fülle von Beet- und Kübelpflanzen sowie ein hellblau lasierter alter Vogelbauer, ein antiker Gartentisch und eine Trockenmauer – all das macht den Garten von Emmanuel de Sauvebœuf so herrlich romantisch.*

A DROITE: *Peut-on imaginer que cette belle maison provençale et son jardin ont vu le jour il y a à peine quatre ans ? Cela tient du miracle.*
DOUBLE PAGE SUI-VANTE: *Des oliviers, une profusion de plantes et de plantes en pot, une vieille cage à oiseaux en bois badigeonnée d'un lavis bleu, une ancienne table de jardin et des murs en pierre sèche composent le jardin romantique d'Emmanuel de Sauvebœuf.*

PREVIOUS PAGES: *Emmanuel is an inveterate collector whose eclectic tastes range from neo-classical plaster statuettes and seashells to antique patchwork, religious icons and oil portraits.*
RIGHT: *The Louis XVI-kitchen is packed with jams and preserves. Traditional Provençal pottery adds a colourful, regional touch to the room.*

VORHERGEHENDE DOPPELSEITE: *Emmanuel ist Sammler aus Passion. Ob klassizistische Gipsbüsten, Muscheln, alte Patchworkdecken, sakrale Statuen oder Porträts – ihn fasziniert alles.*
RECHTS: *In den Louis-XVI-Wandschränken der Küche stapeln sich unzählige Marmeladengläser. Provençalische Fayencen geben dem Raum eine bodenständige Note.*

DOUBLE PAGE PRECEDENTE: *Emmanuel est un collectionneur invétéré. Qu'il s'agisse de plâtres d'académie néo-classiques, de coquillages, d'anciens patchworks, de statues religieuses ou de portraits, tout l'enchante.*
A DROITE: *Dans les placards de style Louis XVI de la cuisine s'entassent d'innombrables pots de confiture. Les faïences provençales ajoutent une note de couleur et de terroir.*

L'ATELIER DES LAUVES

Paul Cézanne

Aix-en-Provence

"Young Marie has just been in to clean my studio. It's finished now and I'm moving in bit by bit," Paul Cézanne wrote to his niece, Paule Conil, on 1 September 1902. The grand master of Aix could finally paint in peace and quiet, shut away in his spacious 'atelier' on the upper floor of a modest country house surrounded by trees and greenery. It was here on the outskirts of Aix, in his studio on the Chemin des Lauves, that the painter came to create his unique artistic universe dominated by still lifes of his favourite accessories: bottles, a plaster statue of Cupid, an assortment of human skulls and that famous earthenware bowl full of apples. It was here that he painted his superb "Bathers," laying the canvas flat on the floor and peering down at it from the top of a ladder to inspect progress. Cézanne died in Aix, in his apartment on the Rue Boulegon, on 22 October 1906, and silence descended on the studio where he had once dreamt of "conquering Paris with an apple." It was the writer Marcel Provence who saved the studio and its contents for posterity. And it was thanks to an American project masterminded by the late John Rewald that the Lauves studio finally opened its doors to Cézanne fans in 1954.

LEFT: *Cézanne's walking stick and the hat which the artist wore come rain, wind or shine, still hang in their customary places.*

LINKS: *Cézannes Hut, getreuer Gefährte an Wind- und Regentagen, und sein Spazierstock, der ihn auf allen Wegen begleitete, befinden sich noch an Ort und Stelle.*

A GAUCHE: *Le chapeau de Cézanne, fidèle compagnon des jours de vent et de pluie, et la canne qui l'accompagnait lors de ses promenades sont toujours en place.*

„Die kleine Marie hat mein Atelier geputzt, das nun fertig ist und in dem ich mich nach und nach einrichte", schrieb Paul Cézanne am 1. September 1902 an seine Nichte Paule Conil. Endlich hatte der Künstler Ruhe zum Malen in seiner geräumigen Werkstatt im obersten Stock eines bescheidenen Landhauses. Im Atelier am Chemin des Lauves am Rande von Aix schuf Cézanne sein Universum, insbesondere die Stillleben mit seinen liebsten Accessoires – Flaschen, ein Gips-Cupido, Totenköpfe und die unvermeidliche Fayenceschale mit Äpfeln. Hier entstanden die herrlichen „Badenden": Seine Fortschritte prüfte er von einer Leiter aus, während die Leinwand flach auf dem Boden lag. Als Cézanne am 22. Oktober 1906 in seiner Wohnung in der Rue Boulegon in Aix starb, wurde es still im Atelier des Mannes, der sich vorgenommen hatte, „Paris mit einem Apfel zu erobern". Dem Schriftsteller Marcel Provence verdanken wir, dass Atelier und Inhalt überdauerten. Durch eine amerikanische Initiative unter Leitung von John Rewald konnte das Atelier des Lauves 1954 seine Pforten wieder öffnen – für alle Cézanne-Verehrer und diejenigen, die einen Augenblick lang in sein magisches Universum eintauchen möchten.

Red shutters and pale lemon walls bathed in the golden sunlight of Provence.

Rote Fensterläden und hellgelbe Wände fangen das goldene Licht der provençalischen Sonne ein.

Volets rouges et murs jaune pâle reflètent la lumière dorée du soleil de Provence.

An umbrella hangs from the porcelain handle on the back of the studio door, as if the master had just stepped out for a moment.

Der Regenschirm am Porzellanknauf der Ateliertür scheint auf seinen Herrn und Meister zu warten.

Le parapluie accroché au pommeau en porcelaine de la porte de l'atelier semble attendre le maître.

« La petite Marie a nettoyé mon atelier qui est terminé et où je m'installe peu à peu », écrit Paul Cézanne le 1er septembre 1902 à sa nièce Paule Conil. Le maître d'Aix peut maintenant peindre en toute tranquillité, dans un vaste atelier au sommet d'une modeste maison de campagne entourée de verdure. Dans son atelier du chemin des Lauves, en bordure d'Aix, Cézanne va se construire un univers où domineront des natures mortes composées avec ses accessoires préférés – des bouteilles, un cupidon en plâtre, quelques crânes humains et l'incontournable coupe en faïence remplie de pommes. Il y créera ses sublimes « Baigneurs », inspectant du haut d'une échelle leur évolution sur la toile couchée à même le plancher. Cézanne meurt à Aix, le 22 octobre 1906 dans son appartement de la Rue Boulegon et le silence descend sur l'atelier de celui qui rêvait de « conquérir Paris avec une pomme ». C'est à l'écrivain Marcel Provence que nous devons la survie de l'atelier et des objets. Et c'est grâce à une initiative américaine présidée par feu John Rewald que l'atelier des Lauves a ouvert ses portes en 1954 aux admirateurs de Cézanne et à tous ceux qui veulent, l'espace d'un moment, se plonger dans son univers magique.

ABOVE: *Simple and stripped of all ornamentation, Cézanne's humble studio reflected the artist's need for solitude and silence.*
RIGHT: *The door is always open to Cézanne enthusiasts who wish to spend a few moments in the place where the artist created so many of his masterpieces.*
FACING PAGE: *The interior has been reconstructed with a painstaking eye to detail. Even the most ordinary corner of the room houses a still life which could have been composed by Cézanne himself.*

OBEN: *Mit seiner bescheidenen, schmucklosen Atmosphäre erfüllte das Atelier Cézannes Bedürfnis nach Einsamkeit und Stille.*
RECHTS: *Die Tür ist stets offen für Bewunderer des Malers, die für ein paar Minuten an dem Ort verweilen möchten, an dem viele seiner Meisterwerke entstanden.*
RECHTE SEITE: *Alles wurde mit erstaunlicher Präzision rekonstruiert. Noch die banalste Ecke ähnelt einem Stillleben, wie es der Maler selbst hätte schaffen können.*

CI-DESSUS: *Modeste, dépouillé de tout ornement, l'atelier de Cézanne répondait parfaitement à son besoin de solitude et de silence.*
A DROITE: *La porte est toujours ouverte aux admirateurs du peintre venus passer quelques instants à l'endroit où naquirent nombre de ses chefs-d'œuvre.*
PAGE DE DROITE: *Tout a été reconstruit avec une précision remarquable. Même le coin le plus banal nous offre l'image d'une nature morte que l'artiste aurait pu composer.*

The Atelier des Lauves
contains everything the
artist needed to compose
his famous still lifes. It
is a moving experience
walking round the stu-
dio and finding the
fruitbowls, skulls, wine
bottles and plaster
cherub standing un-
touched.

*Das Atelier am Chemin
des Lauves enthält alles,
was der Künstler für
seine Stillleben benö-
tigte. Bewegt erkennt
der Besucher Schalen,
Totenköpfe, Flaschen
und den Gips-Cupido,
die er auf seinen Bil-
dern verewigte.*

*L'Atelier des Lauves
renferme tout ce dont
le peintre avait besoin
pour composer ses natu-
res mortes. On recon-
naît avec émotion les
coupes, les crânes, les
bouteilles et le chérubin
en plâtre qu'il a immor-
talisés sur ses toiles.*

FACING PAGE: *The artist's palette, his paint-box and his wooden manikin lie in a corner near an 18th-century screen from his parents' house, Jas de Bouffan.*
RIGHT: *The tall wooden easel stands by the window with its back to the light. The old cast-iron stove in the corner kept Cézanne warm through long winter days.*

LINKE SEITE: *Palette, Malkasten und Glieder-puppe des Künstlers neben einem Paravent aus dem 18. Jahrhundert, der schon in seinem Elternhaus, dem Jas de Bouffan, stand.*
RECHTS: *Die große Staffelei am Fenster steht mit dem Rücken zum Licht. Der guss-eiserne Ofen wärmte den Maler an kalten Wintertagen.*

PAGE DE GAUCHE: *Sa palette, sa boîte à couleurs, son manne-quin articulé se languis-sent. Le paravent 18ᵉ vient de la maison de ses parents, le Jas de Bouffan.*
A DROITE: *Près de la fenêtre, le grand cheva-let tourne le dos à la lu-mière. Le poêle en fonte a réchauffé le peintre pendant les froides jour-nées d'hiver.*

RIGHT: *A still life of apples and onions, arranged in the folds of a tea towel, has been carefully reconstructed on the table.*

FOLLOWING PAGE: *It is thanks to John Rewald's passion and admiration for Cézanne that this magical place has survived intact. If it had not been for Rewald's dedication and generous donations from American enthusiasts, the artist's studio would have fallen into ruin.*

RECHTS: *Auf dem Tisch stellt man liebevoll Stillleben mit Äpfeln und Zwiebeln nach. Unverzichtbar: das in Falten gelegte Geschirrtuch.*

FOLGENDE DOPPELSEITE: *Der Bewunderung John Rewalds für Cézanne verdanken wir die genaue Rekonstruktion dieser magischen Stätte. Ohne seine Hingabe und die großzügigen Spenden seiner vielen amerikanischen Verehrer wäre der Ort mit Sicherheit nicht so erhalten worden.*

A DROITE: *Sur la table on a reconstruit méticuleusement les natures mortes aux pommes et aux oignons, sans oublier les plis du torchon.*

DOUBLE PAGE SUIVANTE: *C'est à l'admiration et à la passion de John Rewald pour Cézanne que nous devons la reconstitution exacte de cet endroit magique. Sans son dévouement et sans les fonds généreux des nombreux admirateurs américains, il aurait connu un sort déplorable.*

$\mathcal{L}$A PASSION D'UN COUPLE

Le Pays d'Aix

This couple appear to be perfectly matched. He is passionate about contemporary art and she echoes this passion with a boundless enthusiasm of her own. He is a best-selling author and organiser of art events and she talks animatedly about her gallery, recounting anecdotes about the fascinating relationships she maintains with icons of the contemporary art world. While the two of them cherish the artistic heritage of their native America, both have a deep-seated love of Provence and they enjoy living in general anonymity in their magnificent residence in the heart of the Aix region. Secluded as it is in splendid isolation, one can spend hours driving around looking for the house. Then it suddenly comes into view at the end of a long and dusty road, glimpsed behind a beautiful wrought-iron gate: a tall 18th-century house, resplendent with ochre walls and surrounded by acres of luxuriant grounds. Could there be anything more delightful than strolling through its spacious salons, pausing to admire the collection of major 20th-century artworks? Could there be anything more indulgent than lingering in this sun-soaked countryside, dominated by the silhouette of Mont Sainte-Victoire? Every bit as glorious as a Cézanne landscape!

LEFT: *A painting by A.R. Penck hangs above a console table decorated with a collection of lion figures (a reference to the owner's astrological sign: Leo).*

LINKS: *Ein Gemälde von A.R. Penck über einer Konsole mit einer von vielen Löwenfiguren (Löwe ist das Sternzeichen des Hausherrn)*

A GAUCHE: *Un tableau de A.R. Penck audessus d'une console qui accueille de nombreuses effigies de lions (le signe du zodiaque du maître de maison).*

Er ist, wie er selbst sagt, Liebhaber zeitgenössischer Kunst und sie schließt sich seinem rückhaltlosen Enthusiasmus an. Zudem ist er Bestsellerautor und Organisator künstlerischer Events. Sie spricht mit leuchtenden Augen von ihrer Galerie und erzählt Anekdoten von ihrem faszinierenden Austausch mit den Größen der aktuellen Kunstszene. Für das künstlerische Erbe ihrer Heimat Amerika begeistern sich beide, betonen jedoch auch ihre aufrichtige Liebe zur Provence und das Glück, auf ihrem bildschönen Anwesen bei Aix-en-Provence ganz anonym und für sich sein zu dürfen. Sie haben guten Grund, ihr herrliches Domizil geheim zu halten. Man muss schon lange, lange suchen, bis man es findet: Dann plötzlich erscheint am Ende eines staubigen Feldwegs hinter einem dekorativen schmiedeeisernen Zaun eine ockerfarbene Villa aus dem 18. Jahrhundert inmitten eines prachtvollen Parks. Gibt es etwas Schöneres, als in diesen geräumigen Salons zu leben, umgeben von einigen der glanzvollsten Kunstwerke des 20. Jahrhunderts – noch dazu in diesem herrlichen, sonnendurchfluteten Eckchen Provence, in dem schon der nahe Mont Sainte-Victoire an die Landschaften Cézannes erinnert?

A lively work by Keith Haring complements the pure vertical lines of a radiator.

Ein lebhaftes Bild von Keith Haring hängt über einem Heizkörper mit strenger Linienführung.

Un très beau tableau de Keith Haring est accroché au-dessus d'un radiateur aux lignes sévères.

Il se dit passionné par l'art contemporain et elle fait écho à son enthousiasme sans bornes. Il est aussi auteur de livres à succès et organisateur d'événements artistiques. Et elle parle avec animation de sa galerie, rapportant des anecdotes sur les rapports fascinants qu'elle entretient avec les icônes de l'art contemporain. S'ils s'enflamment tous les deux pour l'héritage artistique de leur Amérique natale, ils avouent aussi leur amour inconditionnel de la Provence, proclamant le bonheur qu'ils éprouvent à vivre dans l'anonymat de leur magnifique demeure au cœur du pays d'Aix. Ils ont toutes les raisons du monde de jeter le voile du mystère sur leur belle demeure. Il faut chercher longtemps, très longtemps pour la trouver. Mais soudain, au bout d'une route poussiéreuse et derrière une jolie grille en fer forgé, une haute maison 18e couleur ocre, entourée d'un magnifique parc, apparaît dans toute sa beauté resplendissante. Peut-on être plus heureux que dans ces vastes salons où l'œil s'attarde sur des œuvres majeures de l'art du 20e siècle ? Et peut-on se sentir mieux que dans ce beau pays inondé de soleil où la proximité de la Montagne Sainte-Victoire évoque la splendeur des paysages peint par Cézanne ?

Four silk-screen prints by Andy Warhol form a striking quartet in the master bedroom.

Über dem Doppelbett der Hausherren hängen vier Serigrafien von Andy Warhol.

Au-dessus du lit des maîtres de maison on reconnaît quatre sérigraphies signées Andy Warhol.

ABOVE: *It is impossible to conceive of a Provençal garden without the gentle play of a fountain and a stretch of water.*

RIGHT AND FACING PAGE: *Rigorous geometric forms dominate in both house and garden, where the border is made up of privets pruned into rectangular hedges and spheres.*

FOLLOWING PAGES: *These collectors have proved that they have an exceptional eye for contemporary art and a remarkable talent for setting it off in their interiors.*

OBEN: *Ein provençalischer Garten ohne Wasserbecken und plätschernden Brunnen ist kaum vorstellbar.*

RECHTS UND RECHTE SEITE: *Geometrische Strenge dominiert im Haus und auch im Garten: Die Beete sind mit Ligusterhecken und Kugelbäumchen gestaltet.*

FOLGENDE DOPPELSEITE: *Die Sammler haben einen ausgezeichneten Blick für zeitgenössische Kunst und das Geschick, sie perfekt in ihre Wohnräume zu integrieren.*

CI-DESSUS: *Le jardin provençal est inconcevable sans le murmure d'une fontaine et la vue d'un plan d'eau.*

A DROITE ET PAGE DE DROITE: *Rigueur géométrique pour cette maison et son jardin dont le parterre est formé de troènes taillés en haies ou en boule.*

DOUBLE PAGE SUIVANTE: *Les collectionneurs ont prouvé leur œil exceptionnel pour l'art contemporain et un talent remarquable pour l'intégrer à leur intérieur.*

FREDERIC MECHICHE

Hyères

Those familiar with Frédéric Méchiche's work admire the way his décors blend the beautiful and the ephemeral with a quest for the perfect finishing touch. The French interiors maestro is notorious for his design 'volte-face.' One minute Méchiche will be experimenting with an 18th-century French flavour, the next he is seized with a sudden burst of 1940s nostalgia. This will, in turn, be usurped by an urge for 60s design. As fervent Méchiche followers rush to decorate their homes in pure Georgian style, the maestro is already one step ahead, trawling the antique markets and vintage design boutiques in search of a fibreglass chair by Verner Panton! As groupies put the finishing touches to their sumptuous 'Madame du Barry' décor, Méchiche is negotiating for a pair of brushed steel wall lamps from the 1970s. Who would have imagined that one day Méchiche would bring his passion for metamorphosis to bear on a small fisherman's house, tucked away in a narrow alleyway in the heart of old Hyères? In his home, Méchiche has replaced Louis XVI medallion chairs with Harry Bertoia classics, covered the walls' ancient patina with Le Corbusier-style white paint and banished wood and earthenware in favour of metal and plastic. "My version of Provence!" he declares.

Wer Frédéric Méchiche gut kennt, weiß, dass sich in seinen Dekorationen nicht nur Schönheit, sondern auch Qualität und Vergänglichkeit manifestieren. Nicht selten trifft man den Meister mitten in einer seiner berüchtigten Kehrtwendungen an: Innerhalb kürzester Zeit sind die 1940er Jahre out, das französische 18. Jahrhundert in, jedoch nur, um schon bald wieder von den „swinging sixties" abgelöst zu werden. Während seine Anhänger noch eifrig dabei sind, sich georgianisch einzurichten, durchstreift Méchiche schon wieder die Flohmärkte und verhandelt mit Kennern des Vintage-Stils über einen Glasfaserstuhl von Verner Panton! Und während seine Groupies noch in einem Dekor schwelgen, das einer Madame du Barry würdig wäre, ist Frédéric schon stolzer Besitzer von einem Paar Wandlampen aus gebürstetem Edelstahl im Stil der 70er. Selbst vor seinem Fischerhäuschen in der Altstadt von Hyères macht sein Bedürfnis nach ständigen Metamorphosen nicht Halt. Stühle von Harry Bertoia machen Louis-XVI-Sesseln Platz, klösterliches Weiß, das Le Corbusier so sehr schätzte, übertüncht uralte Patina, Plastik und Metall ersetzen Holz und Terrakotta. „Auch das ist die Provence", begeistert sich Méchiche.

In the entrance hall, a graphic artwork by Jean-Charles Blais dominates the perspective.

Im Eingangsbereich dominiert ein von Jean-Charles Blais signiertes Werk den Raum mit seiner grafischen Präsenz.

Dans l'entrée une œuvre signée Jean-Charles Blais domine la composition avec sa forte présence graphique.

Ceux qui connaissent bien Frédéric Méchiche savent que les décors qu'il imagine allient parfaitement la beauté, le souci de la qualité et l'éphémère. Il n'est d'ailleurs pas rare de surprendre le maître durant une de ses volte-face : en peu de temps le style des années 1940 peut détrôner le 18ᵉ français avant de devoir subitement céder la place à la dictature des « sixties ». A l'heure où ses adeptes fervents achèvent de se meubler en pur « Georgian », Méchiche fréquente déjà les Puces et les spécialistes du « vintage » design, à la recherche d'une chaise en fibre de verre signée Verner Panton ! Et alors que ses « groupies » viennent de réaliser un décor digne de Madame du Barry, Frédéric est le fier acquéreur d'une paire d'appliques très « seventies » en acier brossé. Qui aurait cru que sa fièvre de la métamorphose s'abattrait aussi sur sa petite maison de pêcheur située dans une ruelle étroite du vieux Hyères ? Des chaises de Harry Bertoia viennent de chasser les fauteuils à médaillon Louis XVI, le blanc monacal si cher à Le Corbusier couvre les patines à l'ancienne, et le plastic et le métal remplacent le bois et la terre cuite. « Ça aussi, c'est la Provence » s'écrie Méchiche.

The staircase has not been modernised in any way. The charm of its whitewashed walls and uneven steps have survived intact.

Die Treppe wurde nicht aufgearbeitet, sondern durfte den Charme ihrer unregelmäßigen Stufen vor weiß gekalkten Wänden bewahren.

L'escalier n'a pas subi de cure de jouvence et a gardé le charme de ses murs blanchis à la chaux et de ses marches irrégulières.

PREVIOUS PAGES:
*Directoire armchairs
and 'toiles de Jouy' fab-
ric have been replaced
by a stylish 1950s garden
chair, a Knoll coffee
table and a carefully
chosen collection of
artwork. On the roof-
top terrace an Altuglass
table complements a 70s
sofa strewn with Verner
Panton-style cushions.*
RIGHT: *In the guest-
house, Méchiche has
gone in for a timeless
minimalist look based
on a simple black and
white colour scheme.*

**VORHERGEHENDE
DOPPELSEITE:** *Ein
Gartenstuhl aus den
1950ern, ein Couchtisch
von Knoll und einige
ausgewählte Kunstwer-
ke sind an die Stelle von
Directoire-Sesseln und
Jouy-Stoffen getreten.
Auf der Terrasse ergänzt
ein Plexiglastisch die
Couch aus den 70ern
und die Kissen im Stil
Verner Pantons.*
RECHTS: *Bei dem kleinen Gästehaus entschied
sich Méchine für zeit-
lose Schlichtheit in
Schwarz und Weiß.*

**DOUBLE PAGE PRE-
CEDENTE:** *Une chaise
de jardin des années
1950, une table basse
signée Knoll et quelques
œuvres d'art bien choi-
sies ont remplacé les fauteuils Directoire et les
toiles de Jouy. Sur la
terrasse une table en
Altuglas, une banquette
«seventies» et des cous-
sins style Verner Panton.*
A DROITE: *Pour la
petite maison d'amis
Méchiche jugea la palet-
te blanc et noir et la
sobriété intemporelle.*

ABOVE: *In the bedroom, Méchiche combines a classic-looking bed draped in white linen with an Altuglass console topped by a 60s lamp.*

RIGHT: *The pure lines of these accessories form their own minimalist still life in a corner by the window.*

FACING PAGE: *An antique cross is juxtaposed with an Altuglass table and a 1960s lamp and chair set off in an 18th-century décor. Méchiche has proved his audacity by taking the best of each era.*

OBEN: *Im Schlafzimmer blieb Frédéric, trotz Plexiglastischchen und 60er-Jahre-Lampe, dem weiß bezogenen Doppelbett treu.*

RECHTS: *Am Fenster findet sich ein minimalistisches Stillleben aus puristisch geformten Objekten.*

RECHTE SEITE: *Ein altes Kruzifix, ein Plexiglastischchen, eine Lampe und ein Sessel aus den 1960ern in einer Umgebung aus dem 18. Jahrhundert. Méchiche gelang ein Stilmix mit dem Schönsten aus der jeweiligen Zeit.*

CI-DESSUS: *Dans sa chambre à coucher, Frédéric est resté fidèle au grand lit drapé de lin blanc et a choisi pour l'accompagner une console en Altuglas et une lampe « sixties ».*

A DROITE: *Près d'une fenêtre, une nature morte minimaliste avec des objets aux formes pures.*

PAGE DE DROITE: *Une croix ancienne, une console en Altuglas, lampe et siège des années 1960 dans un décor 18ᵉ — Méchiche a réussi ce mélange en choisissant le meilleur de chaque époque.*

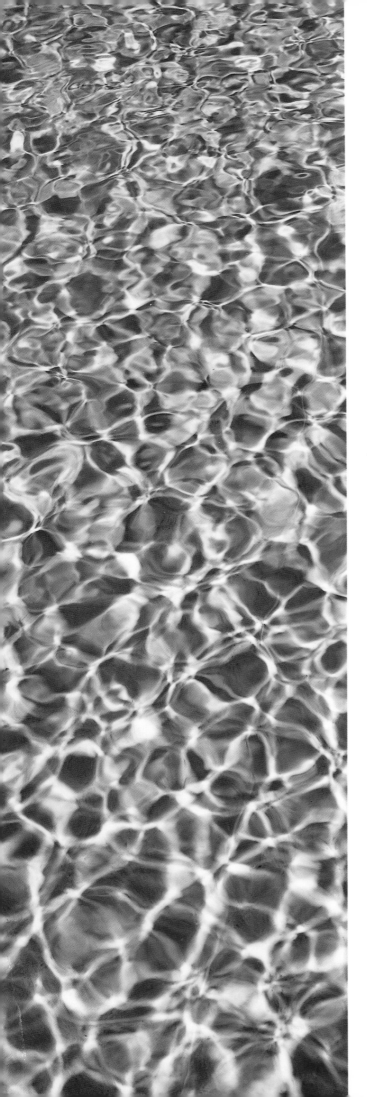

VILLA BELLEVUE

Jan & Monique des Bouvrie

Baie des Canoubiers

Jan des Bouvrie's renown as a designer and interior architect has spread far beyond his native Netherlands. In collaboration with his wife, Monique, a passionate advocate of audacious forms and colour, Jan has developed a signature interior style based on minimalism, pared-down design and the omnipresence of his favourite colour, white. Des Bouvrie has long been an ardent admirer of the Provence and the laidback lifestyle of the Midi and always regretted selling his villa near Saint-Tropez. So when he saw this magnificent Belle Epoque villa offering sweeping views across the Baie des Canoubiers, he bought it without a moment's hesitation. The designer admits his impulsive gesture ended up costing him dearly, for when he first laid eyes on the Villa Bellevue it was little more than a magnificent ruin. What's more, the villa's elaborate columned balcony and ochre façade were diametrically opposed to his design tastes. However, Jan managed to impose his Huguenot signature on the Bellevue, adding two new wings, a swimming pool and a spacious terrace, and painting the façade and interior white. The new-look Villa, filled with contemporary artwork and furniture designed by des Bouvrie himself, now dominates the bay in all its Hollywood-style splendour.

LEFT: *The reflection cast by the sun in the swimming pool has the allure of a contemporary artwork.*

LINKS: *Das vom Schwimmbecken reflektierte Sonnenlicht gerät zu einem natürlichen modernen Kunstwerk.*

A GAUCHE: *Les reflets du soleil dans la piscine créent un tableau contemporain composé par la nature.*

Sein Ruf als Designer und Innenarchitekt reicht weit über die Grenzen der Niederlande hinaus. Unterstützt wird er von seiner Frau Monique, die ganz auf gewagte Farben und Formen setzt. Der schöne hugenottische Name des Bouvrie steht für Interieurs, die sich durch Klarheit und allgegenwärtiges Weiß auszeichnen. Jan liebt die Provence und ist fasziniert von der unaufgeregten Lebensweise des Midi. Der Verkauf seiner Villa bei Saint-Tropez tat ihm später so Leid, dass er keinen Augenblick zögerte, als man ihm eine große Belle-Epoque-Villa mit atemberaubendem Blick über die Bucht von Canoubiers anbot. Heute räumt des Bouvrie ein, dass ihn seine spontane Zusage viel Geld gekostet hat, denn so schön das Haus auch aussah, so war es doch damals eine Ruine. Mit ihrem säulenverzierten Balkon und der ockerfarbenen Fassade entsprach die Villa zunächst nicht Jans Geschmack. Erst mit zwei weiteren Flügeln, einem Pool, einer großen Terrasse und dem durchgehend weißen Anstrich von Fassade und Innenräumen drückte Jan dem Haus seinen Stempel auf. Heute enthält die Villa eine Fülle zeitgenössischer Kunst und vom Hausherrn selbst entworfener Möbel. In prächtiger Hollywood-Manier thront sie hoch über der Bucht.

With its dazzling white walls and its columned verandah, Bellevue looks like a colonial mansion in the Caribbean.

Mit seinem blendenden Weiß und der Säulenveranda erinnert die Villa Bellevue an den karibischen Kolonialstil.

Avec sa blancheur éclatante et sa véranda à colonnes, Bellevue arbore un faux air de maison coloniale style Caraïbes.

Il a acquis une solide réputation de designer et architecte d'intérieur bien au-delà des frontières des Pays-Bas. Secondé par sa femme Monique qui ne jure que par les couleurs et les formes audacieuses, Jan des Bouvrie signe de son beau nom huguenot des intérieurs qui se font remarquer par leur aspect épuré et par l'omniprésence du blanc, la couleur préférée du créateur. Grand amateur de la Provence et fasciné par la vie décontractée que l'on mène dans le Midi, il a toujours regretté d'avoir vendu sa villa du côté de Saint-Tropez. Lorsqu'on lui a proposé une grande villa Belle Epoque offrant une vue époustouflante sur la Baie des Canoubiers, il n'a pas hésité une seconde. Aujourd'hui, Des Bouvrie avoue que son geste impulsif lui a coûté cher. Jolie ruine, mais ruine quand même, la villa Bellevue avec son balcon orné de colonnes et sa façade ocre ne ressemblait en rien au style qu'il affectionne, mais en ajoutant deux ailes, une piscine et une grande terrasse, et en peignant la façade et l'intérieur en blanc, Jan y a apposé sa signature. Aujourd'hui, la villa est remplie d'œuvres de l'art contemporain et de meubles créés par son propriétaire et domine la baie de toute sa splendeur hollywoodienne.

Jan has constructed a small terrace behind the house, enclosing the private space with four low walls.

Hinter dem Haus ließ Jan eine kleine Terrasse anlegen und mit vier halbhohen Mauern einfassen.

Derrière la maison, Jan a construit une petite terrasse en entourant l'espace restreint de quatre murs bas.

Des Bouvrie built his swimming pool against the stunning backdrop of the Baie des Canoubiers. Set between luxuriant palm trees, the pool becomes a stage and the terrace a balcony overlooking the natural theatre décor.

Des Bouvrie baute seinen Pool mit Blick auf die atemberaubende Baie des Canoubiers. Eingefasst von prachtvollen Palmen wird das Becken zum Podium, die Terrasse zum Balkon und das Ganze erscheint wie ein Bühnenbild.

Des Bouvrie a placé sa piscine face à la splendide Baie des Canoubiers. Limitée par des palmiers luxuriants, la piscine devient un podium, la terrasse un balcon et l'ensemble un décor de théâtre.

ACKNOWLEDGEMENTS

DANKSAGUNG

REMERCIEMENTS

We have neither the words nor the space to express our deep gratitude to all those who so warmly welcomed us during our trips to Provence. We would, however, like to make special mention of the hospitality offered by France Louis-Dreyfus, Jean Claude Brialy, Timothy Hennessy, Siki de Somalie, the Stein family, John Burningham and Helen Oxenbury. We would also like to thank Michel Fraisset and the town council of Maillane, who gave us free access to Cézanne's atelier and to the house of Frédéric Mistral. Thanks to them, "Lou souléou me fai canta" (the sun makes me sing).

Uns fehlen die Worte und auch der Platz, um allen zu danken, die uns während unseres Provence-Aufenthalts so herzlich empfangen haben. Dennoch möchten wir die Gastfreundschaft von France Louis-Dreyfus, Jean Claude Brialy, Timothy Hennessy, Siki de Somalie, der Familie Stein, John Burningham und Helen Oxenbury nicht verschweigen. Dank gebührt auch Michel Fraisset und dem Bürgermeisteramt in Maillane, die uns den Zugang zu Cézannes Atelier und zu dem Haus von Frédéric Mistral ermöglicht haben. Dank ihres Entgegenkommens „Lou souléou me fai canta" (Die Sonne brachte mich zum Singen).

Les mots et l'espace nous font défaut pour exprimer notre gratitude à tous ceux qui nous ont chaleureusement accueillis pendant nos séjours en Provence. Nous ne pouvons toutefois omettre de mentionner l'hospitalité que nous ont offerte France Louis-Dreyfus, Jean Claude Brialy, Timothy Hennessy, Siki de Somalie, la famille Stein, John Burningham et Helen Oxenbury, et de remercier Michel Fraisset et la Mairie de Maillane qui nous ont donné libre accès à l'atelier de Cézanne et à la maison de Frédéric Mistral. Grâce à eux, « Lou souléou me fai canta ».

Barbara & René Stoeltie

© 2005 TASCHEN GmbH
Hohenzollernring 53, D–50672 Köln
www.taschen.com

© 2005 for the works of Keith Haring:
The Estate of Keith Haring
© 2005 for the works of A.R. Penck:
Galerie Michael Werner, Cologne
© 2005 for the works of Andy Warhol:
Andy Warhol Foundation for the Visual
Arts/ARS, New York

Concept, edited and layout by
Angelika Taschen, Berlin
Design by Catinka Keul, Cologne
General project management by
Stephanie Bischoff, Cologne
Text editing and coordination by
Christiane Blass, Cologne
English translation by Julie Street, Paris
German translation by Birgit Lamerz-
Beckschäfer, Datteln

Printed in Italy

ISBN 3–8228–2527–1
(Edition with English/German cover)
ISBN 3–8228–2528–x
(Edition with French cover)

PAGE 2: *In François Halard's house, the sun cannot penetrate the jalousie shutters.*
SEITE 2: *Im Wohnhaus von François Halard gelingt es den Sonnenstrahlen nicht, durch die Fensterläden zu schlüpfen.*
PAGE 2: *Dans la demeure de François Halard le soleil n'arrive pas à se faufiler entre les volets à jalousies.*

PAGE 4: *Garlic drying against the wall, a typical Provençal scene.*
SEITE 4: *Knoblauch hängt zum Trocknen an der Wand: typisch für die Provence.*
PAGE 4: *De l'ail que l'on a mis à sècher contre le mur : image typique de la Provence.*

PAGE 198: *Paul Cézanne, Cherries and Peaches (detail), 1883/87. Oil on canvas, 50 x 61 cm, Venturi 498. County Museum of Art, Los Angeles, CA.*
SEITE 198: *Paul Cézanne, Stillleben mit Kirschen und Pfirsichen (Detail), 1883/87. Öl auf Leinwand, 50 x 61 cm, Venturi 498. County Museum of Art, Los Angeles, CA.*
PAGE 198: *Paul Cézanne, Cerises et pêches (détail), 1883/87. Huile sur toile, 50 x 61 cm, Venturi 498. County Museum of Art, Los Angeles, CA.*

Photo Paul Cézanne: © Artothek, Weilheim.

TASCHEN'S
HOTEL BOOK SERIES
Edited by Angelika Taschen

"'Decorator porn,' a friend calls it, those sensuous photograph books of beautiful houses. Long on details and atmosphere and packed with ideas, this is a bountiful look at beautiful but unpretentious homes in the place where 'everything is founded on the link between beauty and well-being.' It's easy to linger there."
The Virginian-Pilot, USA

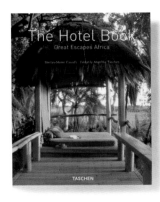    

  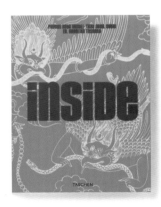 

IN PREPARATION:
The Hotel Book
Great Escapes North America
The Hotel Book
Great Escapes Central America
The Hotel Book
Great Escapes City
Hotels by Famous Architects
Island Beauties

TASCHEN'S
LIVING IN SERIES
Edited by Angelika Taschen

IN PREPARATION:
Living in the Caribbean
Living in the Desert
Living in Japan

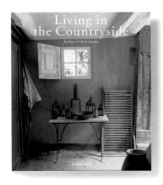  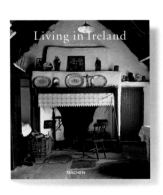 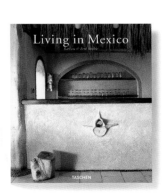 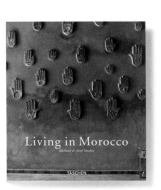